Better Homes and Ga

HALLOWEEN
Decorating • Entertaining • Projects

TABLE
CONCO

of
TIONS

4 SUMMON A SPELL

6 Pumpkins on Parade · 22 Haunting Your Home

34 SCARE UP SOME FUN

36 Treats Incognito · 44 Scare-able Wearables · 52 Bewitching Decorations

58 GATHER THE GHOULS

60 What's Brewing? · 64 Eerie Edibles · 68 Fright-Night Delights

72 Groan-Ups' Halloween Party

76 TRICKS & TREATS

78 Patterns · 86 Recipes

SUMMON

a spell 11

6   Pumpkins on Parade

22   Haunting Your Home

PUMPKINS on PARADE

Whether it's a fun and festive Halloween you seek or something a bit more frightening, count on autumn's plethora of pumpkins to help cast a magical spell.

A Lumina pumpkin *makes a perfect canvas for a jovial man-in-the-moon portrait in gray acrylic, opposite. Painting this guy is easier and safer than carving, and he'll last longer than a jack-o'-lantern. The patterns begin on page 78.*

The paleness of this carved Jarrahdale, *above, makes his candlelit orange-tone insides stand out. His pupils were cut from a white Lumina pumpkin.*

An unusual carving technique *gives this pumpkin, left, a checkerboard glow. To duplicate it, etch just the skin of the pumpkin without going all the way through the shell. The deeper you cut, the more light will shine through.*

After a few simple facial features are carved out, this guy's face is gouged with jagged cracks to make rivulets of wrinkles. His bad-hair-day look comes from a shock of willow branches (choose dried ones from a crafts store or fresh from your garden). Drill small holes into the pumpkin top to easily insert the branches.

The simply features on this pumpkin are perfect for a first-time carver. A quarter-moon smile is studded with garlic-clove teeth, and each arched eye holds a radish; everything is attached with florist's pins. Use an apple corer to "drill" holes for hair and ear placement; fill with broccoli stalks and artichokes. The whimsical gourd nose is held in place with toothpicks.

Mix and match cut shapes from different colors of pumpkins for a custom look. Scoop out the insides, and use a template to cut identical shapes out of two different pumpkins. It's important that the pieces you exchange are exactly the same size.

To turn pumpkins into vases, remove the tops and hollow out the insides. Place a watertight container inside the pumpkins to keep your flowers fresh and the pumpkins from getting soggy.

Mr. Mummy will have you wrapped tight with fear when his black marble eyes fall on you.

Use letters or words etched into a tower of pumpkins, right, to send your guests a spooky message. Carve one letter or word per pumpkin, and stack the pumpkins on a dowel to create a tower. Or scatter your pumpkins along an entryway to spread out your greeting. Use our photos as a guide to trace the letters freehand. Scrape off just enough of the the pumpkin skin to set off each letter or word.

MR. MUMMY

MATERIALS
Marking pen
Paring knife
Smooth white pumpkins
Spoon or ice cream scoop
Two flat toothpicks
Two black marbles
Strong glass adhesive such as E6000
Candle

INSTRUCTIONS
Draw a line around the pumpkin top. Cut off the top as shown in Photo 1, *below*. Scoop out the insides as shown in Photo 2.

Cut the following slits using the photograph, *opposite*, for inspiration: two for the eyes (wide and tall enough to accommodate the marbles), one for the nose, and one for the mouth. Cut more slits around the pumpkin and on the edges of the lid.

Place a toothpick vertically in each eye opening where the marbles will go. Glue a marble to each toothpick. Let dry.

Note: Never leave a burning candle unattended or within the reach of children.

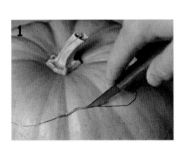

GROW YOUR OWN PUMPKINS
Raise your own bumper crop with seeds from these sources:

■ Cotton Candy and 'Rouge Vif d'Etampes' seeds are available from Local Harvest; www.localharvest.org.

■ Lumina and Baby Boo seeds are available from W. Atlee Burpee & Co., 300 Park Ave., Warminster, PA 18974; 800-888-1447; www.burpee.com.

■ Jarrahdale, Jack Be Little, and Baby Boo seeds are available from Geo. W. Park Seed Co., Inc., 1 Parkton Ave., Greenwood, SC 29647; 800-213-0076; www.parkseed.com.

■ Baker Creek Heirloom Seed Co., 2278 Baker Creek Rd., Mansfield, MO 65704; www.rareseeds.com.

■ Seeds From Around the World, 3421 Bream St., Gautier, MS 39553; www.seedman.com.

PERFECT PAINTED PUMPKINS

To paint a pumpkin, try these tips:

■ Test latex or acrylic paints on a hidden spot on the pumpkin. Pumpkins have a waxy surface that repels some paints.

■ Use a latex primer if you want to change the color of the pumpkin.

■ After the primer has dried, brush or spray a coat of paint on the entire pumpkin. For deeper color, apply a second coat.

■ Paint designs with latex or acrylic paint using a fine-tip artist's brush. Or try an acrylic paint pen for greater control.

■ Age the surface with an antiquing stain. Apply a coat of polyurethane to protect the painted design and to make the pumpkin shine.

Give your pumpkin an unusual twist by putting words in its mouth, above. When the pumpkin glows in the night, your message to Halloween revelers will come shining through.

Battery-powered lights put the glow inside this Halloween greeting, left. The words warn visitors to think twice before entering your domain. Setting these cautionary pumpkins on your front steps or along a walkway ensures that only the bravest trick-or-treaters will make it to your door.

With its ghostly pallor, what else could this Lumina pumpkin be but the missing head of that legendary Sleepy Hollow horseman? The pumpkin's smooth surface sports the lanky schoolmaster's name in black acrylic paint, complete with all the flourishes of pen-and-ink calligraphy.

PUMPKIN-CARVING BASICS

MATERIALS

Fresh pumpkin or artificial carvable pumpkin

Pumpkin-carving tools (including assorted saws and
   drills, a poker, and a scoop)

Wood-carving set (including gouges)

Clay tools for engraving and cutting grooves
   or a kit

Flat-edge ice cream scoop or large serving spoon

Apple corer, grapefruit spoon, crafts knife, clay
   tools, or other appropriate tools to get the
   look you want

Tracing paper, tape or straight pins

Pins, toothpick, and/or adhesives

Petroleum jelly

INSTRUCTIONS

Most artificial pumpkins come with an opening in the base and are hollow and ready to carve. *Note: For safety, never use a candle inside an artificial pumpkin; use an electric or battery-powered light. Warn children to stay away from candles, and keep any fabric decorations away from pumpkins containing candles.*

Prepare fresh pumpkins: If you plan to carve a fresh pumpkin, draw the outline of a six-sided lid on top of the pumpkin. Then draw a notch at the back to use as a guide for replacing the lid. Make the lid opening large enough to easily clean out the pumpkin. Instead of cutting a lid, you may wish to draw a round opening on the bottom of the pumpkin. With the bottom removed, the pumpkin can sit over a candle or light.

Cut out the lid or bottom opening with a saw or a knife (Photo 1). To cut out a lid, carve at an angle toward the pumpkin center. This creates a ledge to support the lid. To cut out a bottom opening, cut straight into the base.

Clean out the seeds and pulp with a scoop or a spoon (Photo 2). Scrape the pulp from the area you plan to carve until the wall is about 1 inch thick (Photo 3).

For fresh and artificial pumpkins: Choose a pattern, and enlarge or shrink the design as needed to fit your pumpkin. Attach the pattern to your pumpkin using tape or straight pins. If you use pins, place them on the design lines to avoid unwanted holes in the pumpkin.

For a fresh pumpkin, use a poker tool to make holes along the design lines about 1/8 inch apart (Photo 4). Don't push the poker all the way through the wall of the pumpkin; remove the

pattern. For an artificial pumpkin, use a pencil to draw firmly over the pattern and engrave the design lines on the pumpkin skin.

Cradle the pumpkin in your lap, and use a crafts knife or a saw to begin cutting out the design (Photo 5). For smaller, more intricate designs, use a fine-tooth saw for carving. Grasp the saw as you'd hold a pencil, and cut with a continuous up-and-down motion, keeping the saw perpendicular to the pumpkin. Apply only gentle pressure to avoid breaking the knife or saw blade and to guard against stressing or breaking the pumpkin. To avoid putting pressure on areas already carved, work from the center of the design outward. Remove and reinsert the knife to make corners; don't twist the blade. Use your finger to carefully push the pieces out of the pumpkin.

To create an interesting design with color and light, you can remove the skin of the pumpkin after cutting out all openings. Use a rounded gouge, assorted clay tools, a grapefruit spoon, or a crafts knife to remove the skin and pulp to the thickness desired (Photo 6).

To use a candle with a fresh pumpkin, place the candle inside and carefully light it after all carving is completed. Let the candle smoke blacken a spot on the lid, and use a saw to cut a 1-inch-diameter hole for a chimney at that spot to vent the smoke and heat. To reduce shriveling, coat the cut edges of your carvings with petroleum jelly. You can revive a shriveled pumpkin by soaking it in water for 1–8 hours. After removing it from the water, let it drain and dry it carefully.

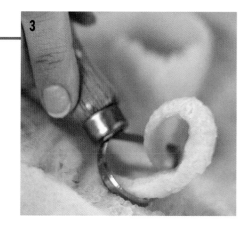

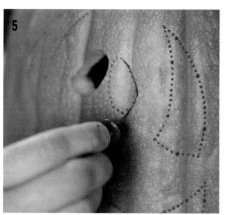

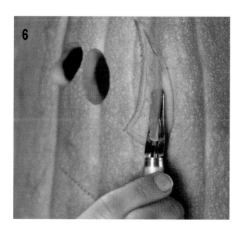

Greet your guests at the door with a pumpkin house-number sign. Stack small, medium, and large Cinderella pumpkins (removing the stems, except for the top one), and trace stenciled number outlines using a crafts knife. Then scrape the pumpkin skin out of the stenciled numbers, revealing the lighter pumpkin flesh underneath.

Carve a haunted house using a large pumpkin as the house and a smaller one for the front entry. Pie pumpkins carved with pickets ring the house like a glowing fence. Use battery-powered lights (available at hobby stores); they'll last longer and are safer than candles.

CARVING TIPS

Create pumpkin designs using wood-carving tools for scraping, cutting, and scooping and crafts knives for detailed carving and etching, *left*. Create the patterns on paper first; tape the paper patterns to the pumpkin, and trace the lines using a pen. Remove the pattern, and use a crafts knife to cut along the depressions made by the pen. To make patterns for words or names, use various computer fonts. The art is in the carving. Cut away just the rind for a design that glows golden when lit from the inside. Or cut all the way through the pumpkin wall to catch the flicker of candlelight.

An old quilt pattern inspired this patchwork design. After applying a base coat of cream-color latex paint, create the pattern by masking off squares and painting a top coat of khaki. Slightly adjust the pattern around curves. The patterns begin on page 78.

RUSTIC CANDELABRA

MATERIALS

Antique rake

Sharp knife

Miniature pumpkins

Votive candles

Metal skewer or ice pick

18-gauge wire

Wire cutters

INSTRUCTIONS

Secure the rake handle in the ground. Cut the tops off the pumpkins. Discard the lids. Cut out areas large enough to accommodate a votive candle.

Using a metal skewer or ice pick, punch two or three small holes around the top edge of each pumpkin.

Cut two or three equal lengths of 18-gauge wire. Thread one length through each hole, twisting to secure. Bring the loose ends of wire together and loop them around the rake tines; twist to secure. Insert a candle in each pumpkin.

Note: Never leave a burning candle unattended or within the reach of children.

Fashion an outdoor pumpkin candelabra *from an antique wooden garden rake, above. Suspend the pumpkins from wire hangers. See complete instructions at left.*

Add some twinkle in the night with your own lighted pumpkin patch. Drill holes in the tops of several of the pumpkins, insert battery-powered candles, and create an interesting mound. Stripe the tapers with black and orange electrical tape.

When it's time for summer's flowers to give way to harvesttime decorations, turn a pair of urns into statuesque pedestals for an arrangement of monogrammed pumpkins, right. Begin by choosing a font for the letters in a word-processing program on your computer. Then simply print them out at the desired size, and use them as patterns to cut out the letters.

PUMPKINS WITH PERSONALITY

A true pumpkin aficionado wouldn't ask for "a pumpkin" any more than a connoisseur of fine wine would shop for "some champagne." Instead, picky pumpkin people look for one with the perfect flavor and consistency for cooking, or just the right shape or color for carving or painting. Here are some favorite varieties to get you started.

SMALL ORANGE (2 to 5 pounds): Sugar (good for pies), Baby Bear (flattened shape), Spooktacular (bright orange), Frosty (smooth skin), Winter Luxury (good for cooking).

MEDIUM ORANGE (8 to 15 pounds): Autumn Gold (best of its kind) and the common, dependable jack-o'-lantern.

LARGE ORANGE (15 to 25 pounds): Jumpin' Jack (tall, dark, and handsome), Big Autumn (yellow-orange), Ghost Rider (dark orange).

GREEN: Jarrahdale (pretty sage color; very flavorful).

RED: Cinderella (resembles Cinderella's carriage; deep red-orange, flattened shape).

TAN: Buckskin (good for canning; butternut flavor).

VARIEGATED: Green-Striped Cushaw, Sweet Potato.

WHITE: Casper, Lumina, Little Boo, Snowball (all medium-size; generally smooth skin; great candidates for painting).

MINIATURE: Baby Boo (white), Sweetie Pie (scalloped), Munchkin, Jack-Be-Little.

BUMPY: Long Island Cheese.

HEADSTONE ENGRAVINGS

MATERIALS

Sharp knife

Pumpkin

Spoon or ice cream scoop

Tracing paper

Pencil

Transfer paper

Wood chisel

INSTRUCTIONS

Cut the pumpkin down both sides, leaving the front, back, and bottom intact. Scoop out the insides.

Enlarge and trace the desired pattern on *page 83*. Place the pattern on the pumpkin, and slip a piece of transfer paper between the pumpkin and the pattern. Transfer the lines to the pumpkin.

Use the wood chisel to carve the desired designs into the pumpkin skin.

Give your guests a graven greeting with a pair of frightful pumpkins, below. *The motifs are chiseled into the skin and glow eerily when the pumpkins are lit with a candle from behind.*

Set the stage for an enchanted evening with plenty of pumpkins and vintage-look decorations. The little witch costumes take their cue from sew-easy clown patterns found at fabrics stores. Top off the outfits with pointy hats crafted from black construction paper sprinkled with glitter.

HAUNTING your HOME

Greet Halloween ghosts and goblins with spellbinding decorations in every nook and cranny of your home.

Jeepers creepers! *You can get the peepers, above, by purchasing wooden balls at a crafts store, painting them white, and freehand-painting the details. To make a spooky-looking scrapbook, turn a vintage photo album into a tome of incantations with a handmade bookplate.*

Fashion fallen leaves *into a fantastic garland by using a needle and thread to string them together. Plain wooden pumpkin cutouts from the crafts store painted with simple jack-o'-lantern faces peek out along its length.*

Party favors *become part of the decor when stuffed inside an old bicycle's wire basket alongside a bunch of pumpkins. Prop the bike on the front porch or near the front door so guests can choose a treat as they leave the gathering.*

COME IN AND SIT A SPELL

MATERIALS

Computer and printer

8½×11-inch sheets of wood-pattern scrapbooking paper

Three 4×36-inch pieces of balsa wood

Spray adhesive

12 decorative tacks

INSTRUCTIONS

Type your message in the font of your choice on a computer, adjusting the size so the words are no more than 3½ inches tall. Format the text so each individual word is centered on a separate page. If necessary, adjust the print orientation to landscape so the text runs in the same direction as the wood-grain on the paper. Print each word on a sheet of the patterned paper.

Cut the printed sheets into 4×11-inch strips, centering each word on a strip. Position the words on the balsa wood, referring to the photograph *above*. Cut additional 4-inch-wide strips of the patterned paper with the grain running the length of the strips to completely cover the wood. Spray adhesive onto the backs of the strips, and smooth them in place on the balsa.

Use decorative tacks to mount the signs on stair risers. (If wet weather is a concern, laminate the paper before assembling the project.)

Guests will feel right at home with this friendly invitation—until they realize they've been bewitched! Use a spooky Halloween font like Chiller or Jokeman to create the words on wood-pattern paper. For stability, adhere the printed paper to strips of balsa wood and tack the pieces to the steps. To decorate concrete steps, affix the strips with removable double-stick poster tape.

Cast a candlelit glow on your Halloween festivities with hat-shape lanterns, *left, dressed for the occasion. Vellum and scrapbooking paper turn these plain-glass hurricane lanterns into seasonal treats. Dim the lights for a magical light show.*

HAT-SHAPE LANTERN

MATERIALS

4×6-inch or 4×8-inch glass-hurricane
    lantern with glass bottom
12×12-inch sheets of two coordinating
    patterned scrapbooking papers
Lightweight black paper
Spray adhesive
Crafts knife
Sheet of orange vellum
Computer, printer, and white paper
Crafts glue
Pinking shears
Black poster board
Circle cutter (optional)
Candle

INSTRUCTIONS

Measure the height and diameter of the lantern; subtract 1/8 inch from the height. Use these measurements to cut a piece of patterned paper and black paper. Spray the back of the patterned paper with adhesive; press onto the black paper. Use a crafts knife to cut a diamond-shape opening in the papers.

Type the word you want on a computer, sizing it to fit inside the diamond opening; print it on vellum. With the word centered, cut the vellum slightly larger than the opening; glue to the black side of the layered papers.

Cut 1/2-inch-wide strips of black paper to frame the diamond opening. Trim one edge with pinking shears. Glue the strips along the front edges of the opening with the pinked edges toward the printed word.

Spray the black side of the layered papers with adhesive; mount to the outside of the lantern with the bottom edges even. The paper should be slightly shorter than the lantern so it's not a fire hazard.

Spray the back of a coordinating patterned paper; mount it on black poster board for the brim. Measure the diameter of the lantern bottom. Cut a circle from the layered brim papers 3 inches larger than this measurement. Pink the edge. Glue the bottom of the lantern centered on the brim.

Cut a 1-inch-wide strip of coordinating paper to fit around the lantern base. Pink the top edge. Spray the back side with adhesive. Adhere to the lantern bottom with the bottom edge touching the brim. Insert the candle.

FRONT-PORCH GHOSTS

MATERIALS

For each ghost:

7-foot length of clothesline wire

Padded clothes hanger

Two 3-foot lengths of polyethylene foam
    pipe insulation to fit 3/4-inch pipe

Heavy-duty clear packing tape

Bubble wrap

Plastic-foam wig form

Glue gun and hotmelt adhesive

20-pound-test fishing line

Recycled white dress with tulle or other
    sheer flowing fabric (look for old prom
    or wedding dresses at thrift stores)

Latex, rubber, or white fabric gloves

Cotton balls

Translucent trash bags: 1/2-mil or less

White masks (optional)

Screw eyes, nails, or pushpins (for flying ghost)
    or tall candelabra (for standing ghost)

INSTRUCTIONS

For the arms, wrap the center of the clothesline wire six times around the padded area of the hanger so an equal length of wire extends beyond each of the hanger's ends. Slide a piece of pipe insulation over each end of the wire and up onto the padded area of the hanger. Use packing tape to connect and secure the pipe insulation at the center of the clothes hanger.

Straighten the hanger hook. For the torso, drape a piece of bubble wrap in the desired length over the hanger, letting it fall over the front and back of the hanger. Push the straightened hook through the wrap. Add as many layers of bubble wrap as needed for fullness. Tape the front layers to the back just below the hanger. Insert the straightened hook into the center bottom of the plastic-foam wig form; hot-glue in place. Use tape and glue to secure the head to the torso.

Arrange the dress or fabric on the assembled body. To aid in assembly, suspend the ghost with fishing line at the neck and each arm. Attach enough extra line to accommodate the ghost's final location and height. Shred and tear the dress with a pair of scissors, cutting off some pieces of the fabric. Glue strips of the torn fabric to the head for hair. Cut the arms to the desired length. Stuff the fingers and hands of the gloves with cotton balls. Slip the stuffed gloves onto the arms and secure with tape.

For fabric gloves, bend and glue the fingers in place. Drape the arms with torn fabric; glue in place. Continue to tear and attach fabric for a ghostlike effect. Cut, shred, and tear pieces of the trash bags and glue on where needed to fill out the figure.

Bend the arms to the desired shape. Place a white mask on the head if desired. For a flying ghost, insert screw eyes, hooks, or pushpins into the soffit or ceiling and suspend the ghost with fishing line. Use extra lengths of fishing line to prevent it from spinning. For a standing ghost, drape the ghost over a tall candelabra and secure with tape.

An all-white welcome puts a ghostly pallor on the porch, below. Silky fabric ghosts hung at different heights with fishing line wave eerily in the breeze, and a scattering of white pumpkins lines the porch steps. If white pumpkins aren't available, spray-paint orange ones instead.

Light up the night *Halloween-style with orange and black luminarias, right. Even young trick-or-treaters can make these cheerful lights with a little help from an adult.*

TIN-CAN LUMINARIAS

MATERIALS
Tracing paper
Clean empty tin cans
Permanent marker
Hammer and large nail
Ruler
Wire
Spray paint: orange and black
Tea-light candles

INSTRUCTIONS
Using tracing paper, trace the pumpkin face or bat patterns, *page 83,* or make your own design. Transfer the pattern of your choice to a clean tin can; go over the transferred pattern with a permanent marker. Fill the tin can with water; place it in the freezer. When the water in the can is frozen, remove the can from the freezer.

Use a hammer and nail to punch the design in the can. Punch two holes in the rim of the can on opposite sides, centering the design between the two holes. Let the ice melt; allow the can to dry completely.

Cut a 16" length of wire. Insert one end of the wire into a hole in the rim; twist the end of the wire around the wire length. Insert the other wire end through the opposite hole, securing it in the same manner.

Spray-paint the pumpkin can orange and the bat can black. Let the paint dry. Place a tea-light candle inside each can, and hang securely from a branch or garden hook.

A VISIT TO A PUMPKIN FESTIVAL
When autumn rolls around, people who live in cooler climates like to get out and enjoy the warm sunny days of fall. A visit to a pumpkin farm or festival in your town or a neighboring community can be lots of fun for you and your family.

At a farm, children get to choose their own pumpkin for carving. They can search pumpkins in a variety of colors—they aren't just orange anymore—and a variety of sizes.

Pumpkin festivals (and some farms) offer many activities geared to families. Some of most popular: costume contests, largest-pumpkin contests, pumpkin-carving contests, pumpkin-pie-eating contests, corn- and hay-field mazes, wagon and hay rides, petting zoos, and entertainment such as musical groups and plays.

Some festivals also have haunted houses, amusement rides, and arts and crafts fairs connected with them. And since everyone gets hungry, food abounds at pumpkin festivals. You won't go home hungry after eating your way through the traditional festival fare—funnel cakes, corn dogs, cotton candy, and kettle corn. At many of the festivals, you'll also find a variety of foods prepared from pumpkins—pies, butters, fudge, cookies, soups, breads, and more.

The white color of a Lumina pumpkin works perfectly for a funny skeletal-looking face, left. Miniature Baby Boo, Jack-Be-Little, and Sweetie Pie pumpkins become perfect candleholders when hollowed out to fit votives and placed on old garden tools. Always be cautious when placing candles near leaves. For safety, keep them at least 6 inches away.

Whether hanging from the bough of a tabletop tree or around a doorknob, these glittery star ornaments, opposite, shine brightly. Recycle old postcards with Halloween-theme images to serve as the centers, and attach a bell at each point. You'll get a cheery jingle whenever the wind blows.

Turn an old country table into a beggar's banquet. Purchased paper lanterns add to the merriment.

STAR ORNAMENTS

MATERIALS

Vintage-look Halloween graphic
Acrylic circle to fit in center of star
Photo spray adhesive
Purchased 9- or 12-inch star
Crafts glue
Paintbrush
Glitter: black or orange
Tinsel: black or orange
Hole punch
12-inch piece of 1/4-inch-wide ribbon
5 gold jingle bells

INSTRUCTIONS

Cut a circle from a Halloween graphic, such as a photo or postcard, the size of the acrylic circle. Lightly spray the front of the graphic circle with adhesive. Press the adhesive side onto one side of the acrylic circle. Spray the back of the graphic circle with adhesive and center it on the star; press in place.

Apply crafts glue to the front of the star up to the edges of the acrylic circle using a paintbrush. Sprinkle glitter on the wet glue. Let the glue dry. Tap off the excess glitter. Also, apply glitter to the back of the star if desired.

Apply glue along the edge of the acrylic circle. Press tinsel into the glue; let dry. Punch a hole in the top point of the star. Insert the ribbon through the hole, bring the ribbon ends together, and knot them about 1 inch from the ends. Glue a jingle bell at each point of the star; let the glue dry.

PAPER-COVERED TREAT BOX

MATERIALS

6×5-inch-diameter crafts box

12×12-inch sheets of two coordinating
    patterned scrapbooking papers

Spray adhesive

Black poster board

Circle cutter (optional)

Pinking shears

Crafts glue

Tinsel: black or orange

3/4×6-inch crafts stick

Black acrylic paint

Paintbrush

Glue gun and hotmelt adhesive

Purchased star or Halloween glitter cutout

Computer, printer, and white paper
    (optional)

INSTRUCTIONS

Measure the height and circumference of the box; add 1/2 inch to the height. Use these measurements to cut a piece of patterned paper, piecing multiple sheets if needed to reach completely around the box. Lightly spray the back of the paper with adhesive, and mount it on the outside of the box with the bottom edges even. Fold the excess paper to the inside of the box, covering the top edge; press to adhere.

Spray the back of another sheet of the same paper with adhesive, and mount it on black poster board. Measure the diameter of the bottom of the box. Cut a circle from the layered paper-poster board with a diameter 3 inches larger than this measurement. Trim the edges with pinking shears. Glue the bottom of the box, centered on top of the circle. Apply a line of crafts glue along the bottom edge of the box. Press tinsel into

the glue; let the glue dry. Paint the crafts stick black; let the paint dry.

Spray the back of a coordinating sheet of patterned paper, and mount it on poster board. Cut a circle from the layered paper/poster board that's the same diameter as the box. Hot-glue the crafts stick to the paper side of the circle so 3 inches extend beyond the edge.

For the fan, divide the diameter of the box by 2 and subtract 1/4 inch. Use this measurement to cut a 12-inch strip of coordinating paper. For example, the strip for a 6-inch-diameter box would be 2 3/4 inches wide. Beginning at a short edge of the strip, make accordion-style pleats across the paper; finger-crease each pleat. Pinch one pleated edge together for the center of the fan. Glue the short edges of the pleated paper together, forming a circle. Glue the fan, centered, to the layered circle, covering the top of the crafts stick. Center the glitter cutout on the fan and glue. If desired, use a computer to print a Halloween message on white paper for a banner. Cut out the banner and glue it to the glitter cutout.

Hot-glue the crafts stick to the inside of the box at the center back so there's 1 inch between the top of the box and the fan.

If desired, cut enough 2 1/2-inch-wide strips of the box paper to reach around the inside of the box. Spray the backs of the strips with adhesive and press in place inside the box with the top edges of the paper slightly below the top edge of the box.

A round kraft-paper box covered with scrapbooking paper is the foundation for the festive treat box opposite. Keep sweet treats at your fingertips for munching before trick-or-treaters knock at your door, drop one on a neighbor's doorstep for a bit of fun, or give one as a gift to a coworker.

Turn a dollhouse into a tabletop haunted mansion, left, by painting it black and adding a few spooky paper details.

SCAREUP

some fun

36 Treats Incognito

44 Scare-able Wearables

52 Bewitching Decorations

Hats off to these chocolate
temptations made from sugar
cones and purchased cookies.
Each cone is filled with candy treats
before it's attached to the cookie
base, making for one sweet surprise.

TREATS INCOGNITO

Halloween costumes aren't just for trick-or-treaters anymore. These tasty treats are all dressed up, too. Can you guess what they're made of? Recipes begin on page 87.

Who knew *a favorite snack-time sponge cake could be transformed into a whimsical wing-flapping owl? Round candy eyes, candy-corn feet, and the black licorice eyebrows and tail make this Hootie Twinkie Owl a treat to eat.*

Finger-lickin'-good apples covered in caramel, chocolate, and nuts are Halloween staples, right. Decorate the plate for the occasion by using double-stick tape to attach wide black ribbon to the rim. Then adhere orange rickrack to the inside of the ribbon so it extends above the plate ribbon.

Oozing with yummy pizza ingredients, the overstuffed snake, below, sports a sinister smile and a long forked tongue. To make him, raise and bake a loaf of frozen bread dough, fill the scooped-out shell, and bake it again before slipping the savory reptile onto a serving platter.

A sugared cat cookie tops off a brownie cupcake, set up on a bed of jellybeans, opposite. Let kids frost and embellish their own jack-o'-lantern cookies for a tasty party activity.

Recipes begin on page 87.

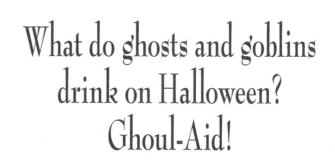

What do ghosts and goblins
drink on Halloween?
Ghoul-Aid!

This skull head will have you white with fright with his piercing black eyes. Surround the cake with gobs of gummy worms for an even more frightening presentation.

Recipes begin on page 87.

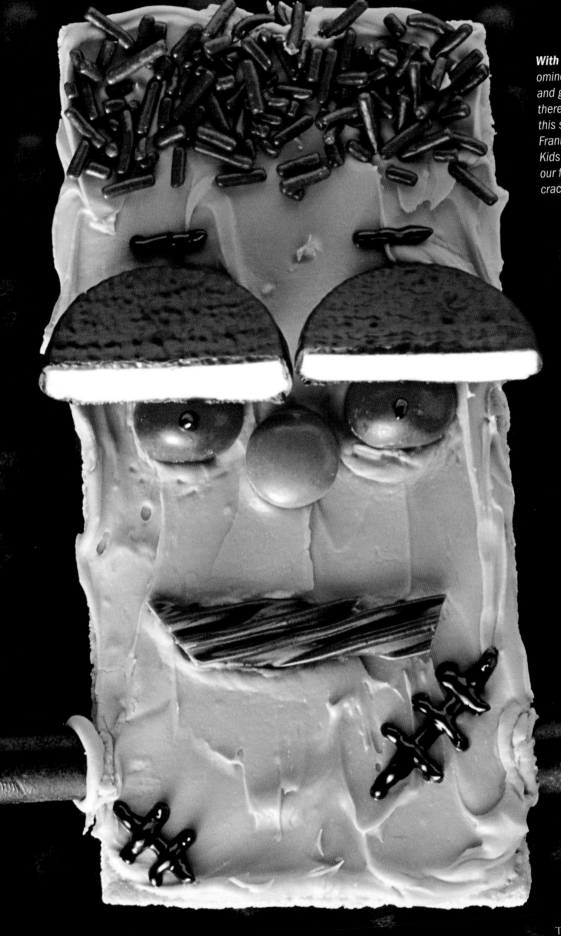

With a green face, ominous neck bolt, and ghastly sutures, there's no mistaking this scary guy—it's Frankenstein's monster! Kids will gobble up our frosted graham-cracker version.

Little ghosts and goblins will delight in decorating the Bats, Rats, Witches, and Cats, *above* and *opposite*, cut from refrigerated cookie dough. Be sure to set out a variety of frosting colors, decorative candies, and colored writing gels for kids to use in fleshing out their creepy creations.

A marshmallow ghost rises from the depths of a mug of Haunting Hot Chocolate, left. Orange peel and nutmeg give this take on the traditional drink a tasty fall twist.

Recipes begin on page 87.

What could be more fun *than scurrying around as a giant beetle or spider? These imaginative felt costumes, opposite and below,* pull over the head like a shirt and come complete with coordinating hats and visors.

SCARE-ABLE WEARABLES

Beetles, spiders, and bats— oh my! Kids love costumes and at Halloween the more fun the better. Your little trick-or-treaters will love this collection of one-of-a-kind costumes and treat bags.

HALLOWEEN BEETLE AND SPIDER COSTUMES

MATERIALS

FOR BOTH COSTUMES:

Measuring tape; scissors

Newspaper for pattern; adhesive tape

Fabri-Tac adhesive fabric glue

Tracing paper

FOR THE BEETLE:

Felt: green and other assorted colors

Stiff felt: black (for legs)

Toy construction hat: yellow

Sharp knife

Two 2½-inch-long plastic-foam eggs
   (such as Styrofoam brand)

Decoupage medium

Tissue paper: red and black

Glue gun and hotmelt adhesive

Two ³/8-inch-diameter wiggle eyes

Two squiggle drinking straws

FOR THE SPIDER:

Clear vinyl

Paintbrush; acrylic paint: white

Felt: orange, black, and beige

Elastic: black

Plastic visor: black

Tissue paper: black

Mod Podge decoupage medium

Plastic-foam balls (such as Styrofoam
   brand): two 1½-inch-diameter and
   six 1-inch-diameter

Eight ½-inch diameter wiggle eyes

Glue gun and hotmelt adhesive

GENERAL INSTRUCTIONS

Take the child's measurements as follows: Extend arms straight out and measure from wrist to wrist (this is the pattern width). Measure from neck to ankle for the back panel length and from neck to waist for the front panel length. Add the measurements together (this is the pattern height). Measure the distance from shoulder to shoulder.

Make the patterns as follows: Cut and tape newspaper together until you have a rectangle that measures the same width and height as established above. Refer to the Cutting Diagrams on *page 85* to mark the neck and shoulder measurements on the pattern. Fold the pattern in half the long way. For beetle and spider, draw designs as shown on diagrams. Trace the beetle leg pattern on *page 85* onto tracing paper; enlarge on a copier and cut out. Trace the patterns for the three spider-leg parts on *pages 85* onto tracing paper; enlarge on a copier and cut out.

BEETLE

Cut the entire beetle body pattern from green felt. Cut out the neck opening, making a vertical slit down the front so the costume will fit over the head.

Cut out the decorative portions from the body pattern; use them to cut out the felt pieces. Glue the pieces to the beetle body.

Cut the leg patterns from stiff felt; glue the legs to the inside of the back panel. To make the legs stick out from the body, cut 1-inch-wide strips of black felt to match the curve of the beetle's back; glue the strips over the legs on the inside back.

Decorate the construction hat with felt pieces, referring to the photo on *page 45* for suggestions. Use a sharp knife to cut plastic-foam eggs in half. Use decoupage medium to cover the large ends (eyes) with red tissue paper and the small ends (antennae) with black tissue paper. Let dry. Hot-glue red eyes to the front of the hat; add the wiggle eyes. Glue the black antennae pieces to the sides. Push straws into the top of the black pieces; secure with glue.

SPIDER

Cut the shape from vinyl. Paint the web on one side of the vinyl back panel. Refer to the photo *opposite*. The paint will bead up to create an airy web effect.

Cut away the web portion of the paper pattern. From black felt, cut out the body, including the front panel. Cut a second (inside back) shape, omitting the front panel. Glue the felt shapes to the vinyl. Cut out the neck opening. Cut a small vertical slit down the front to allow the costume to go over the head. Cut the leg patterns from felt.

Cut decorative pieces from the paper pattern and use them to cut out the felt shapes. Fringe some of the details. Glue the pieces to the front panel; turn the costume over and repeat for the back panel. Match up the body and legs when gluing pieces to the inside. *Note: Do not add details to the inside.*

Cut two wristbands from elastic. Sew the elastic to the wrist area inside the back panel.

Cut out a fang area in the front of the visor. Cut pieces of black tissue paper and use decoupage medium to apply them to all of the plastic-foam balls. Let dry. Glue a wiggle eye to each plastic-foam ball. Hot-glue the finished eyes to the front of the visor. Add fringed strips of beige and orange felt to simulate hair.

Eek! This creepy, crawly spider is sure to snag plenty of Halloween treats in his wicked web. Constructed from vinyl and felt, the costume is even more eye-catching from the back.

BOO-TIFUL BAT COSTUME

MATERIALS

60×60-inch piece of black fabric

White sewing pencil

Scissors

Straightedge

Fusible facing

Elastic

Sequin trim: silver and red

Coordinating threads

Black buttons

Purchased black sweatshirt, black leggings
    or sweatpants, bat ears, white gloves,
    white socks, and plastic fangs

INSTRUCTIONS

Fold the fabric in half to form a triangle. Using the photograph for inspiration, draw curves around the edges of the fabric with the sewing pencil. Cut out the wings through both layers using the diagram, *page 78*. While the fabric is still folded, cut out a center half–circle for the neck. Adjust the size of the cape at the arms and head opening to fit the child. Using a straightedge, draw lines from the curved points to the fold on both the front and back of the costume to form the wing struts.

Fuse the facing inside the neck opening. Make small slits about $1^{1}/_{2}$ inches apart in the neck facing. Thread the elastic through the slits; adjust to fit loosely around the child's neck. Sew the ends together.

Stitch a single row of silver sequin trim along each strut line on the wing front and back. Stitch red sequin trim around the bottom edge. Fit the cape on the child. Sew two sets of black buttons at the underarms through both layers as shown to secure the cape.

Dress the child in the sweat suit, socks, gloves, wings, ears, and fangs.

Wrap fanciful wings around your trick-or-treater as part of this batty getup. Accent the child's cheeks with a dab of face paint and his or her lips with red lipstick.

FELT TREAT BAGS: BASIC BAG

MATERIALS

Felt in the colors indicated for each variation, either 100-percent wool or synthetic

Ruler

Straight scissors

Coordinating threads

Sewing machine

Pins

Pinking shears (optional)

INSTRUCTIONS

Cut two equal-size rectangles from felt. (Our bags range in size from 13×16½ inches to 14×19½ inches.) Using our patterns (*pages 79–81*) or your own designs, appliqué the felt shapes to one of the rectangles, with the design close to the top of the rectangle rather than centered. Lay the appliquéd pieces faceup on the other rectangle, and stitch the rectangles together about ½ inch from the side and bottom edges; leave the top edges open. Use straight scissors or pinking shears to evenly trim each seam allowance to about ¼ inch.

At one bottom corner, adjust the felt layers so part of the bottom seam is directly on top of the side seam. Stitch edge to edge, perpendicular to the existing seams—the farther up from the corner you stitch, the more tapered the bottom of your bag will be. Trim off the corner about ¼ inch from the stitch line, using straight scissors or pinking shears. Repeat this stitching and trimming at the other bottom corner, cutting away an equal amount of felt.

For the handles, sew four 12- to 15-inch-long felt strips into pairs, stitching along both long edges. Evenly trim the edges with straight scissors or pinking shears. Align the ends of the handles along the top inside edges of the bag; pin and then stitch into place.

Send your little ghosts and goblins *out on the town with homemade treat bags that will be remembered long after all the Halloween candy has been devoured. Simply stitch or glue felt shapes to a felt rectangle and then sew the rectangles to one another to create a boxy bottom, with all seam allowances left showing.*

HAUNTED TREE BAG

MATERIALS

Tracing paper

Felt: dark blue, brown, yellow, red, orange, and black

Pinking shears

Straight scissors

Embroidery floss: orange, yellow, and black

Needle

Fabric glue

INSTRUCTIONS

Enlarge the pattern pieces, *page 81*, and trace them onto tracing paper; cut out. Use the pattern pieces to cut the felt shapes as follows.

Cut two 14×19½-inch rectangles from dark blue felt for the bag front and back. Using pinking shears, cut out the tree trunk and leaves. Use straight scissors to cut out the rest of the appliqué shapes.

Stitch the yellow moon to the bag front. Stitch the left trunk panel and stitch in place; overlay the right trunk panel, branches, and tree-trunk center. Sew only along the edges that will show. Referring to the Assembly Diagram on *page 81* for placement, stitch the knothole in a spiral using a length of black embroidery floss. Stitch or glue the bat, spider body, and spider head in place. Hand-stitch the spider legs and web using black embroidery floss. Using orange embroidery floss, make French knots for the spider's eyes.

Glue together the owl body, eyes, beak, and wings. Hand-stitch the feathers using yellow embroidery floss. Glue the owl onto the tree and hand-stitch its orange feet. Secure each leaf to the bag with a contrasting-color running stitch down the leaf center.

Assemble the bag as described in the Basic Bag instructions on page 49, clipping 2½ inches from each bottom corner.

Black thread gives this bag's tree branches a rough barklike appearance, and running stitches let the red and orange leaves flutter in the chilly fall wind.

PUMPKIN BAG

MATERIALS

Tracing paper
Felt: yellow, orange, light green, and black
Pinking shears
Light green embroidery floss
Light green crinkle-texture yarn
Needle
Fabric glue

INSTRUCTIONS

Enlarge the pattern pieces, *page 79*, and trace them onto tracing paper; cut out. Use the pattern pieces to cut the felt shapes as follows.

From yellow felt, cut a 17×14-inch rectangle for the bag front. Using pinking shears, cut out the orange pumpkin panel pieces. Stitch the light green pumpkin stem to the top center of the bag front. Using light green embroidery floss, add running-stitch details. Trim 3/4 inch from the top of the bag so the stem extends beyond the edge. Cut a corresponding rectangle (no stem) for the bag back.

Lay out the large pumpkin panel pieces on the bag with one at the left, one at the right, and one in the center. Referring to the Assembly Diagram on *page 79*, overlap the panel pieces and add the pumpkin center panel piece to the middle, matching the tops of the felt. Remove the pumpkin center panel piece and the center large panel piece, and sew the left and right pumpkin panel pieces to the bag front, stitching just along the outside edges. Add the third large pumpkin panel piece to the center and sew to the bag along the left and right sides only. Add the small pumpkin center panel piece to the middle and stitch to attach. Glue on the face. Join the bag front and back as described in the Basic Bag instructions on page 49, clipping 2 1/2 inches from the bottom corners. Coil and glue green yarn to the front handle. Sew the handle to the right side of the bag front so the yarn "vine" appears to be attached to the pumpkin. Stitch the other handle to the inside of the bag back.

SPIDER BAG

MATERIALS

Tracing paper
Felt: white, black, light green, and red
Transfer paper
Orange embroidery floss
Black chenille yarn
Eight black buttons
Needle
Fabric glue

INSTRUCTIONS

Enlarge the pattern pieces, *page 80,* and trace them onto tracing paper; cut out. Use the pattern pieces to cut the felt shapes as follows.

For the bag front and back, cut two 13×16 1/2-inch rectangles from white felt. Working from the wrong side of the bag front, use transfer paper and a pencil to draw the web design; use orange embroidery floss to outline the web pattern in running stitches.

Cut eight pieces of black yarn in varying lengths for the spider legs. Referring to the pattern and the photo, *below,* for placement, arrange the legs over the web on the front side of the bag front. Glue in place, stopping 1 to 2 inches from the "foot" of each leg. At the point where the gluing stops, secure a black button "knee" over each leg. (The ends of the spider legs hang freely.)

Cut an oval spider body from black felt and stitch it to the bag front, covering the tops of all the legs. Glue on the spider head, eyes, nose, and mouth.

Assemble the bag as described in the Basic Bag instructions on page 49, clipping about 3 inches from the bottom corners and using pinking shears to trim the seam allowances and handles.

Inside this easy-to-make jack-o'-lantern bag, there's plenty of room for even the biggest stash of treats. Adding a whimsical dangling arachnid to the front of our basic felt bag is simple—just use fabric glue.

Your kids' party will
be all abuzz with
these terrific balloons
outfitted to look like a
spider and a beetle,
above and below. *Hang
them above a table,
in a doorway, or give
them away as colorful
party favors.*

BEWITCHING DECORATIONS

Hocus-pocus, alacazam! Use a bit of Halloween magic to turn ordinary household items into extraordinarily fun decorations for a kid-friendly Halloween bash.

BUZZIN' BALLOONS

MATERIALS

Tracing paper; scissors
Sheets of crafts foam: assorted colors
Ruler or tape; hole punch
Glue gun and hotmelt adhesive
9-inch-diameter helium-quality latex balloon
    (one *each* for beetle and spider)
12-inch-diameter helium-quality latex
    balloon (one *each* for beetle and spider)
1.5 mm clear Stretch Magic string (or
    heavy-duty fishing line)

INSTRUCTIONS

BEETLE BALLOON

Note: Cut out all pieces before gluing and assembling the head.

Trace the head pattern on *page 84* onto tracing paper. Make several copies so you can cut them up for pattern pieces. Cut out the head and all features from crafts foam. Cut a 1/2×6-inch strip from yellow foam for the nose. Curl one end of the nose strip and glue the curl in place. Glue all features to the head.

Cut two 1×11³/4-inch connecting head strips from yellow foam. Punch a hole in one end of each strip (1/2 inch from the end). Center the two unpunched ends on the back of the mask. Glue the ends in place. (Do not glue the strips into the hairy portion of the mask.)

Overlap the holes of the connecting strip to form a circle. Thread a 9-inch balloon through both holes with the balloon inside the circle. Blow up the balloon to fit inside the circle; tie a knot in the end.

Trace the leg and wing patterns on *page 84* onto tracing paper; enlarge on a copier and cut out. Cut six legs from green crafts foam and two wings from white crafts foam. Trim the wings with 1/2-inch-wide strips of yellow foam.

Cut two 1¹/2×18-inch connecting body strips from yellow foam. Punch a hole in one end of each strip (about 1/2 inch from the end). Overlap the unpunched ends 1/2 inch; glue together. Make three pairs of tiny slits on each strip half, referring to the diagram on *page 84*.

Thread the end tab of each leg through a pair of slits, starting and ending outside the connecting strip. Glue the tab to the leg. Glue all legs in place. Form the finished strip into a circle, overlapping punched ends. Glue in place.

Cut one 1¹/2×15-inch vertical back brace from red foam, one 1¹/2×18-inch vertical back brace from green foam, and three 1/2×16-inch tummy strips from teal blue foam. Glue the red brace, green brace, and teal blue tummy strips to the inside edge of the body connecting circle, referring to the photo *opposite*. Glue the wings on top of the crossed back braces.

Thread the remaining balloon through the hole in the yellow body connecting circle (with the balloon inside the circle). Blow up balloon to fit within the area you've just made; tie a knot in the end. Tie both the head and body together.

Cut one 1¹/2×11-inch neck strip from yellow foam. Cut a 1/2×9(1/4-inch decorative strip from orange foam. Glue the orange strip to the center of the yellow strip. Make cuts in the strip as shown on the Connecting Body Strip Diagram on *page 84*. Wrap the strip around the neck where you've knotted the balloons together. Join the strip by inserting one slit inside the other. Hang the balloon with Stretch Magic string.

SPIDER BALLOON

Make the head as directed for the beetle balloon. *Note: Cut the connecting head strips from black foam.*

Trace the leg pattern on *page 84* onto tracing paper. Enlarge on a copier; cut out. Cut eight legs from black crafts foam.

From black foam, cut two 1¹/2×18-inch connecting body strips. Punch a hole in one end of each strip (about 1/2 inch from the end). Overlap the unpunched ends 1/2 inch; glue together. Make four pairs of tiny slits on each strip half, referring to the Connecting Body Strip Diagram on *page 84* for assistance. Attach the legs and finish, following the instructions for the Beetle Balloon.

From black foam, cut two 1¹/2×15-inch back braces. Glue the ends of the back pieces on the inside edge of the body connecting circle.

Follow the remaining instructions for the Beetle Balloon, except cut the neck strip from orange foam and omit the decorative strip.

JUMPIN' JACK PIÑATA

MATERIALS

15-inch balloon

2 medium bowls

3 cups white flour

Water

Newspapers

Scissors

Tracing paper

Pencil

Medium-weight colored papers: black,
    purple, yellow, and orange

Crafts knife

Yardstick

Glue stick

Party hat: metallic blue or other color

Paper punch

Silver eyelets and eyelet tool

Lime green plastic lace

2 yards of 1/4-inch-wide ribbon

Darning needle

Crepe paper streamers: orange and green

Small candies or plastic Halloween toys

INSTRUCTIONS

Inflate the balloon and secure with a knot; set the balloon in a bowl.

To make the papier-mâché mixture, pour the flour into a bowl. Stir in water until the mixture reaches the consistency of thick gravy.

Tear newspapers into strips. Dip one strip at a time in the flour mixture. Gently pull the strip between two fingers to remove the excess. Place the wet strip on the balloon as shown in Photo 1, *far left*. Cover the balloon with two or three layers of paper strips, leaving only the balloon knot exposed. Turn the balloon over in the bowl and repeat. Let dry.

Remove the balloon from the bowl. Holding the balloon by the knot, puncture the balloon and remove it from the hardened piñata.

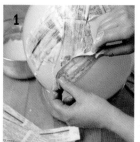
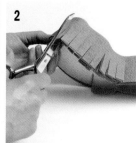

Referring to the photo, *opposite,* draw and cut out facial features and arms from black and yellow papers. Trace around one eye pattern on the small end of the piñata in the eye area. Use a crafts knife to cut out the eye shape 1/4 inch inside the drawn line.

Glue on the black pieces for the yellow eyes and the purple stripes for the hands and legs. Cut a 10-inch circle from black paper for the hat brim. Place the party hat in the center of the paper circle; trace the hat. Cut it out slightly inside the circle. Glue the party hat to the brim. Let dry.

Using the photo as a guide, punch holes along the tops of both shoes. Use an eyelet tool to secure eyelets in each hole. Cut two 24-inch lengths of lime green plastic lace. Lace through the eyelets and tie ends into a bow. Glue the shoes to the legs. Let the glue dry.

Use a crafts knife to cut two small holes in the top of the piñata. Insert ribbon into the needle. Sew through the holes in the piñata top. Remove the needle. Knot the ribbon ends to secure.

Cut 4 yards of crepe paper streamers at a time. Wrap the paper into a 1-foot loop. Carefully cut 1/2-inch-wide fringe along one side of the loop, being careful not to trim through the edges, as shown in Photo 2, *opposite bottom middle.*

Beginning at the bottom (large end) of the piñata, wind and glue the unfringed edge of the crepe paper streamers onto the piñata, as shown in Photo 3, *opposite bottom right.* Continue wrapping and gluing until the piñata is covered. Through the eye opening, fill the piñata with candies or toys.

Pleat the arms. Glue the paper pieces onto the piñata, covering the cutout eye area with a paper eye. Let the glue dry.

Tie a bow from green crepe paper. Glue onto the hat. Let dry.

Made from a papier-mâché- covered balloon, our piñata, opposite, *holds a pumpkin's worth of treats.*

HALLOWEEN PARTY TUB

MATERIALS

Orange enamel spray paint

20-inch-diameter galvanized metal tub

Pencil

Tracing paper

Scissors

Stencil paper

Crafts knife

Adhesive tape

Acrylic paint: black

Stencil brush

Toothbrush

INSTRUCTIONS

Spray-paint the outside of the tub orange. Draw your own face pattern onto tracing paper and cut it out. Transfer the features to stencil paper, and cut them out with a crafts knife. Tape the stencil to the tub, and stencil the face black. Use an old toothbrush to lightly spatter thinned black paint all over the tub.

Thirsty partygoers *can grab their favorite soda from this jovial jack-o'-lantern metal tub. Or fill the tub with water and apples and let kids take turns bobbing away.*

MR. SKINNY BONES

MATERIALS

10-foot length of ½-inch PVC pipe

Hacksaw

Metal file

Scissors

Empty, clean white bleach-bottle for the
    head, about 10 inches tall

2 empty, clean white soap bottles for the
    feet, about 8 inches tall

Black paint marker

½-inch PVC connections: 6—90-degree
    turns for the ribs, 4—45-degree turns for
    the shoulders and hips, 4 cross slips for
    the neck and vertebrae, and 1 T for
    the pelvis

10 yards of white nylon twist rope

White duct tape

8-inch length of 18-gauge wire

Pair of white latex gloves

INSTRUCTIONS

From the PVC pipe, use the hacksaw to
cut two 10½-inch pieces for the lower
legs, two 9½-inch pieces for the upper
legs, two 8-inch pieces for the lower
arms, two 7-inch pieces for the upper
arms, two 6½-inch pieces for the
collarbones, three 4-inch pieces for the
top ribs and the lower back, four 3-inch
pieces for the middle ribs and the hip-
bones, three 2⅓-inch pieces for the
vertebrae, and two 2-inch pieces for the
bottom ribs. File the ends of the pieces
smooth with the metal file.

Use scissors to make a hole in the base
of the bleach bottle and through the front
and back of the soap bottles about 2 inches
from the top. Referring to the photograph,
right, invert the bleach bottle and draw a
face on the side opposite the handle with
the black paint marker.

Referring to the diagram, *page 86,* lay
out the cut PVC pieces and the connections
on the floor or a large table. Fit the pieces

together, sliding the connectors over the
pipe ends. Don't connect the leg and arm
bones yet.

Cut 3-yard and 1-yard lengths of rope,
and wrap the ends with duct tape. Thread
the 3-yard length of rope through the
collarbones until there is an equal amount
of rope extending from the shoulder ends
of the bones. Bend the 8-inch length of
wire to form a hook. Use the wire hook to
pull out the center of the arm rope through
the top of the cross-slip connector. Wrap
one end of the 1-yard length of rope
around the center of the arm rope, and
tape it securely with duct tape. Pull both
ends of the arm rope to bring the center
back into the cross-slip connector. Thread
an upper arm onto each arm rope, and tie
a knot in the rope at the end of each pipe
for the elbow. Thread a lower arm onto
each arm rope and knot the rope below
the pipe, securing a latex glove in each
knot for the hands. Thread the bleach-
bottle head onto the remaining end of the
1-yard rope and tie a knot in the rope
above the head.

Cut a 4½-yard length of rope, and
wrap the ends with duct tape. Thread the
rope through the hip bones until there is
an equal amount of rope extending from
the ends. Thread an upper leg onto each
leg rope, and tie a knot in the rope at
the end of each pipe for the knee. Thread
a lower leg onto each leg rope and then
add a bottle foot; knot the rope below
each foot.

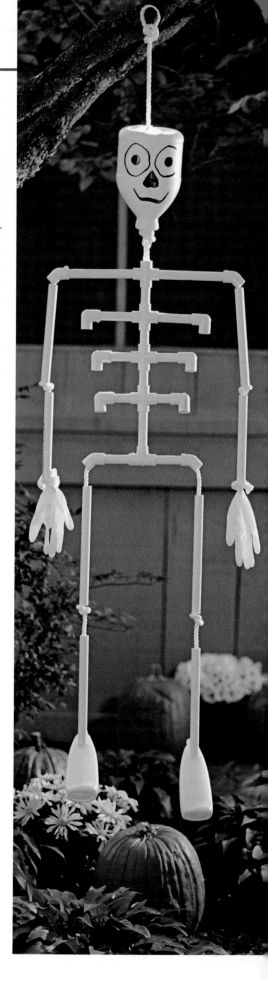

Who* is *that clanking in
the wind? It's just a
smiling skeleton, right,
that you'll enjoy making
from rope, PVC tubing,
and white plastic bottles.

Set the mood for a night of merriment by sending out invitations featuring a grinning black cat or skeleton.

SCARE-ME-SILLY INVITATIONS

CAT INVITE

MATERIALS

Tracing paper

Pencil

Scissors

Craft papers: black, yellow, and white

Glue stick

4×5¼-inch brown kraft postcard

¾-inch round red sticker

Marking pens: silver and black

INSTRUCTIONS

Trace the head-and-face pattern, *page 86,* onto tracing paper and cut out. The silver and black lines will be drawn with marking pens. Trace around the head and pupil patterns on black paper, the eyes on yellow, and the teeth on white. Cut out.

Glue the black head shape to the center of the postcard. Attach the yellow eyes, black pupils, and white teeth. Apply a red sticker to make the nose.

Use a black marking pen to draw in teeth lines, stars, dots, and swirls as shown on the pattern. Use a silver pen to draw in whiskers and lines in the eyes. Color in the stars and one tooth. Make silver dots on top of the black dots and in the center of the swirls.

Write party information on the back of the postcard.

SKELETON INVITE

MATERIALS

Tracing paper

Pencil

Scissors

Craft papers: black, white, orange, and yellow

Ruler

Glue stick

Marking pens: silver and black

Round reinforcement stickers: yellow, purple, and green

Small round green stickers

INSTRUCTIONS

Trace the pattern, *page 86,* onto tracing paper and cut out. The silver and black lines will be drawn with marking pens.

Fold a piece of black paper in half, bringing the short ends together. Trace around the pattern for the card shape on the folded piece of black paper. Trace around the bow-tie shape on orange paper and the skeleton head on white. Cut out the shapes. Cut a 3¾×⅝-inch strip from yellow paper.

Glue the head shape approximately ¼ inch from the top of the card. Use the silver pen to draw in the arms and ribs.

Apply reinforcements and green stickers to the bow tie as desired. Trim or fold under the stickers that hang over the edge of the bow tie. Glue the bow tie to the bottom of the head. Glue the yellow paper strip to the bottom of the card.

Use the black pen to draw in face details and lettering. On the inside, write "AND SOMEWHERE TO GO!" with the silver pen.

Write the invitation information on the inside of the card.

GATHER

the ghouls

60 What's Brewing?

64 Eerie Edibles

68 Fright-Night Delights

72 Groan-Ups' Halloween Party

Who knows what monsters lurk below the surface of a swamp? Dare to drink from this Up-from-the-Depths Swamp Punch and discover a creepy denizen of the deep.

Recipes begin on page 87.

WHAT'S BREWING?

All you need is a pinch of this, a dash of that, and a wave of your magic wand to make these creepy adult-appropriate party drinks. Recipes begin on page 87.

Create the smiling shrunken head for a Shrunken-Head Martini, *below left, from a small onion, whole cloves, and stuffed green olives. Tangles of basil complete the drink, adding whimsy and flavor. Our dramatic Bloody Scary Harry, below right, displays long locks made from beet shreds and a ghoulish star-anise face.*

Small spooky Halloween toys *are up to their ears in the Golden Beetle-Juice Slush, above. Be sure to remove the toys before drinking.*

What would happen *if you concocted a drink with a frog as the main ingredient? Use your imagination with* Frog in a Blender, *near left. Then play mad scientist with our green* Bubbling Brew, *far left, foaming over with a mini-marshmallow surprise.*

Recipes begin on page 87.

Silly but not scary touches on chilled drinks stir up extra fun at any Halloween get-together: *Dracula's Soda (far left), Ghoul-Ade (left), White Ghost (above left), and Layered Ooze (above right).*

A trio of Tombstone Brownies gets its aged granite appearance from a dusting of powdered sugar. The chocolate tombstones are planted in a brownie graveyard with accents of grass made from coconut shavings tossed with green food coloring.

EERIE EDIBLES

Whoever said, "Don't play with your food" hasn't seen this assortment of gooey, ghastly goodies. They're almost as much fun to make as they are to eat. Recipes begin on page 87.

These Eyes of Newt, above, aren't some gross addition to a witch's brew. They're actually made from yummy ingredients that only look disgusting.

An all-time kids' favorite, these adorable chain rattlers, left, have a cereal-and-marshmallow base and are coated with vanilla-flavored candy. Have fun making different ghost shapes and experiment with different candy bits to create a variety of ghoulish expressions.

Greet guests young and old with an enchanting moon-face cookie. Start with a simple sugar cookie recipe, and create the face using our directions, opposite top.

To make Moon Cookies, left *and* opposite, copy a moon face from an old book, and trace the design onto edible rice paper circles using edible-ink pens. Finish decorating with the pens, and attach the circles to sugar cookies with icing.

Chocolate-Licorice Spiderwebs, below, will delight all the ghouls and goblins in your neighborhood, and they're a cinch to make.

To make a spiderweb, place melting chocolate in a plastic zipper bag and heat it in a microwave oven until softened. Arrange six 4-inch pieces of licorice in a star shape on parchment paper. Cut the tip off one corner of the bag, and place a large dot of chocolate in the center of the star shape. Pipe web circles out from the center. Let set for one hour.

HALLOWEEN HISTORY

Halloween is more than 2,000 years old, dating back to an ancient Celtic festival called Samhain. According to some sources, on October 31, the day before the winter season arrived, many people believed ghosts caused trouble among the living. To keep the roaming spirits away, the Celts built roaring bonfires and wore animal costumes.

Hundreds of years later, after Christianity spread and the Church named November 1 All-Saints'—or All Hallows'—Day, Europeans observed a similar tradition by leaving food on their doorsteps to keep ghosts from entering their homes.

This All Hallows' Eve offering was later replaced by the giving out of "soul cakes" during parades to the poor in exchange for their prayers for the dead. Eventually, children began to go door-to-door to collect cakes, apples, and even money. When European immigrants arrived in America in the 1800s, "going-a-souling" turned into what we now call trick-or-treating.

Today the holiday is more about treats than tricks. But in some locales, children still perform a trick, usually reciting a joke they've memorized, to earn their reward on Halloween night.

FRIGHT-Night DELIGHTS

All Hallows' Eve is drawing near, and everything that goes bump in the night is about to crawl out of the woodwork. Black cats, witches, and menacing eyes are all on deck.

Candlelight is perfect *for illuminating the treat table, opposite, while still leaving the yard dark enough for frightfully fun activities.*

To make the eerie tablecloth, opposite and right, simply cut a bolt of fabric with a Halloween pattern to fit your table. Place the fabric over an inexpensive white plastic tablecloth. To make the garland, print your favorite Halloween clip art onto card stock. Cut out the images, punch holes as needed, and string together with orange ribbon.

Dress up plain metal galvanized buckets *by using spray adhesive to attach Halloween-theme party napkins to the outside, opposite and right. (Make sure you scrub the buckets clean inside and out first.) Buy black bat die cuts at a crafts or scrapbooking store and tape them to the handles; then fill the buckets with treats.*

A shadowy glow emanates softly from behind spooky Halloween silhouettes, right. Start with glass hurricane lamps that are open at both ends. Attach a variety of ready-made black die-cut figures and ornate picture frames to the outside of each lamp with double-stick tape. Cover the glass and die cuts with orange vellum paper and secure the edges with "invisible" vellum tape.

HAIR-RAISING TALES

Goose bumps-raising, adrenaline-surging, toe-curling, spine-tingling, bloodcurdling—who doesn't love a good ghost story? "When you're frightened, you kind of know you're alive for a while," says Rick Carson, a full-time professional storyteller who specializes in tales of terror.

To put some scream into your Halloween, Carson offers these tips for telling killer ghost stories.

■ **Pick your stories carefully.** Peruse books or search the Internet. Look for variations on the same story, and don't be afraid to combine them to create your own version. For elementary-school-age children, Carson advises starting with a "slightly creepy" story, moving to a funny one, and finishing with a good jumper.

■ **Get to know your stories.** Practice reading them in front of a group of friends and into a tape recorder.

■ **Set the mood.** Dim the lights, add candles, or use a flashlight to illuminate just your face. You may even want to sit inside a backyard tent or put on a costume.

■ **Let your voice take center stage.** Alter your tone, volume, and pace. Whisper during the really scary parts. "You get quieter so whatever is creeping up on you won't hear you," Carson explains softly, "and it lets the kids pay more attention to you." But be careful. Beginners tend to exaggerate, talking too softly and then too loudly, he says.

This treat-table centerpiece takes on the face of a black cat from a clever arrangement of chocolate-frosted cupcakes and marzipan ears, eyes, and whiskers.

Bring the buffet table to life—as it were—
with deftly spread spiderwebs, charming (plastic)
spiders, candles, pumpkins, and sprigs of red berries.

GROAN-UPS' Halloween PARTY

Just because you're an adult doesn't mean you can't partake in all the Halloween fun. So don a costume, invite a few friends over, and enjoy these appallingly delicious appetizers. Recipes begin on page 87.

This combination of grilled bacon-wrapped shrimp served with a perversely spicey remoulade, *left, is a Faustian temptation few souls could resist.*

Coming to you from way, way South of the Border, *these fiery little packages of delight, below, can be prepared in advance; feel free to make the Hotter-than-Hades Steak and Salsa the day before, and while you're carving, why not groove to "The Monster Mash" to get in the mood?*

In this outrageous canape platter, opposite, the "eyes" truly have it! There's a little something for everyone here, from hearty mini meatballs to fresh mozzarella-and-tomato bites to an elegant grape-and-prosciutto nibble.

Bearing an unsettling resemblance to the real thing, these chicken fingers, right, are going to crawl right off the table onto your guests' plates.

Drive a carving knife through the "heart" of these succulent Adam's Ribs, below, which are seasoned with spicy Jamaican jerk seasoning.

Recipes begin on page 87.

Tricks & Treats

RICKS: patterns

REATS: recipes

TRICKS Patterns

Man-in-the-Moon Pumpkin
(shown on *page 6*)

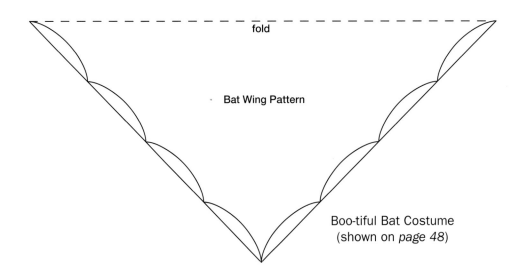

fold

Bat Wing Pattern

Boo-tiful Bat Costume
(shown on *page 48*)

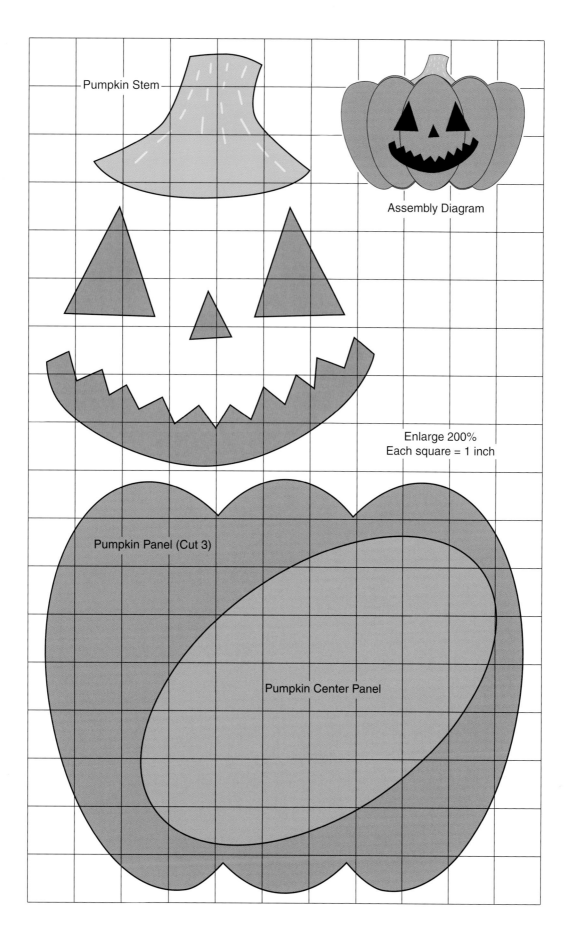

Pumpkin Stem

Assembly Diagram

Enlarge 200%
Each square = 1 inch

Pumpkin Panel (Cut 3)

Pumpkin Center Panel

Pumpkin Bag
(shown on *pages 49* and *51*)

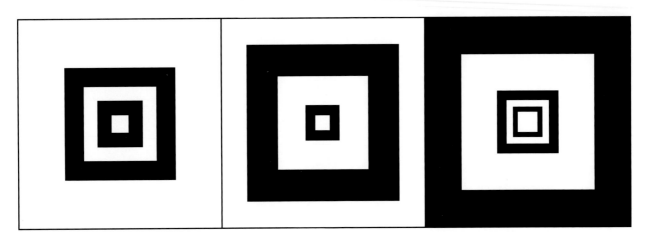

Painted Patchwork Pumpkin
(shown on *page 17*)

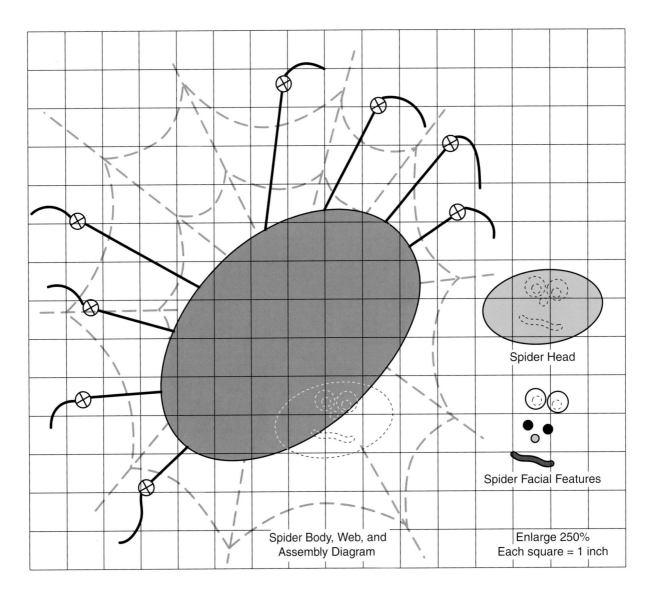

Spider Head

Spider Facial Features

Spider Body, Web, and
Assembly Diagram

Enlarge 250%
Each square = 1 inch

Spider Bag
(shown on *pages 49* and *51*)

Leaves

Owl Facial Features

Owl Wing

Owl Wing

Bat

Branch

Owl Body

Branch

Knothole

Tree Trunk Left

Tree Trunk Right

Moon

Spider Body

Spider Head

Tree Trunk Center

Assembly Diagram

Enlarge 200%
Each square = 1 inch

Haunted Tree Felt Bag
(shown on *pages 49* and *50*)

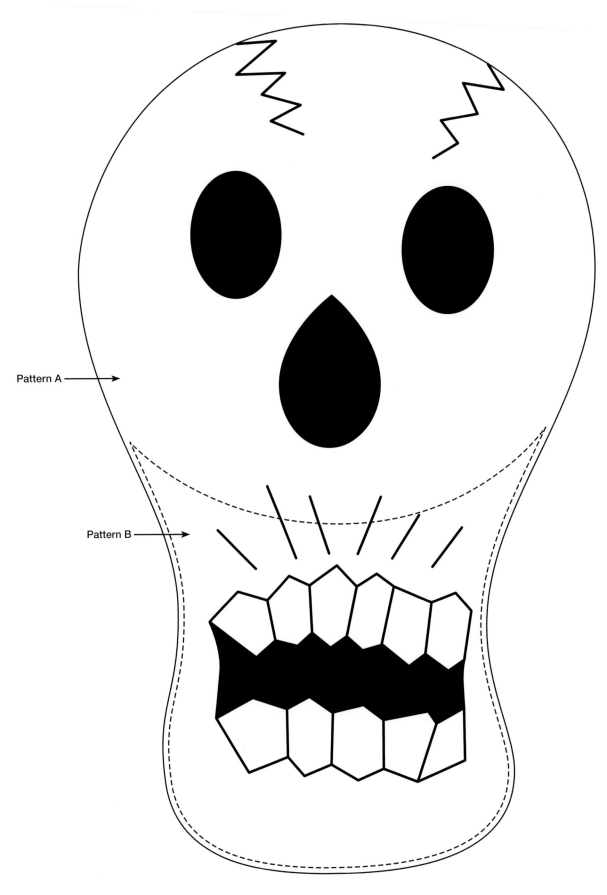

Pattern A

Pattern B

Skull Head Cake (shown on *page 40*)

Tin-Can Luminarias (shown on *page 28*)

RIP Pumpkin Pattern   1 Square = 1 Inch

Boo Pumpkin Pattern   1 Square = 1 Inch

Headstone Engravings
(shown on *page 21*)

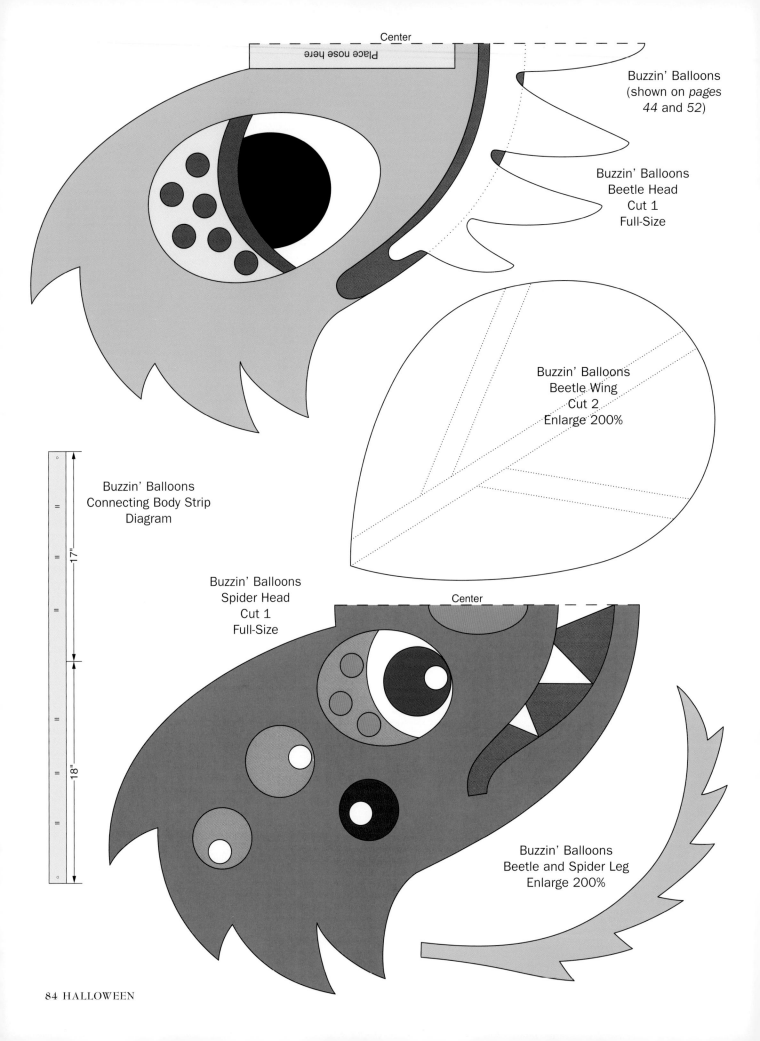

Center

Place nose here

Buzzin' Balloons
(shown on *pages*
44 and *52*)

Buzzin' Balloons
Beetle Head
Cut 1
Full-Size

Buzzin' Balloons
Beetle Wing
Cut 2
Enlarge 200%

Buzzin' Balloons
Connecting Body Strip
Diagram

17"

18"

Buzzin' Balloons
Spider Head
Cut 1
Full-Size

Center

Buzzin' Balloons
Beetle and Spider Leg
Enlarge 200%

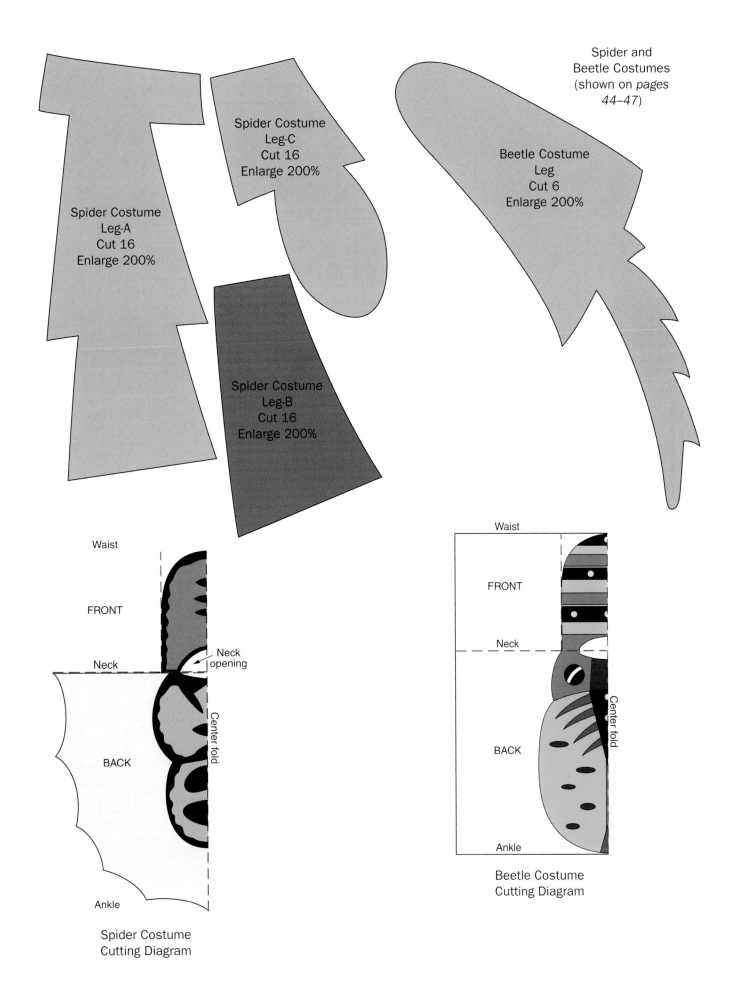

Spider and
Beetle Costumes
(shown on *pages*
44–47)

Spider Costume
Leg-A
Cut 16
Enlarge 200%

Spider Costume
Leg-C
Cut 16
Enlarge 200%

Spider Costume
Leg-B
Cut 16
Enlarge 200%

Beetle Costume
Leg
Cut 6
Enlarge 200%

Waist

FRONT

Neck

Neck
opening

BACK

Center fold

Ankle

Spider Costume
Cutting Diagram

Waist

FRONT

Neck

BACK

Center fold

Ankle

Beetle Costume
Cutting Diagram

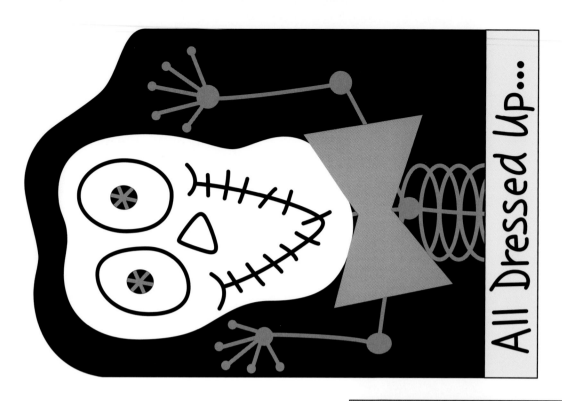

All Dressed Up...

Scare-Me-Silly
Invitations
(shown on *page 57*)

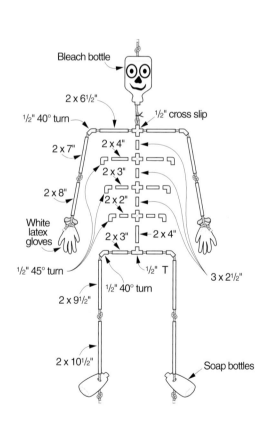

Bleach bottle

2 x 6½"

½" 40° turn · ½" cross slip

2 x 7" · 2 x 4"

· 2 x 3"

2 x 8" · 2 x 2"

White
latex
gloves

2 x 3" · 2 x 4"

½" 45° turn · ½" T

2 x 9½" · ½" 40° turn · 3 x 2½"

2 x 10½" · Soap bottles

Mr. Skinny Bones
Assembly Diagram
(shown on *page 56*)

TREATS Recipes

Scare Up Some Fun

BATS, RATS, WITCHES, AND CATS
(shown on pages 42 and 43)
Start to Finish: 1 hour

1   18-ounce roll refrigerated sugar cookie dough or peanut
      butter cookie dough
1   16-ounce can vanilla frosting
Paste food coloring in desired colors
Large and small purple, black, orange, or green gumdrops
Small decorative candies
Black and purple coarse sugar
Black string licorice
Red, green, and purple edible writing gel

1. Freeze cookie dough for at least 2 hours. Divide frosting among four small bowls. Add desired paste food coloring to each bowl. Cover and set aside.
2. Unwrap frozen cookie dough.
3. To make the Bats: Cut cookie dough into ¼-inch thick slices. Make a jagged cut through the center of a slice as shown in Photo 1, *below left*. Carefully separate the two pieces. Space cookies about 2 inches apart. Bake in a preheated oven (refer to package instructions for temperature) for 7 to 9 minutes or until edges are lightly golden. Cool on wire racks. Decorate as desired, or frost with black-tinted frosting. Cut a small black gumdrop in half and place in the center of the wings for ears. Sprinkle cookies with desired sugar. Add small candies for eyes.
4. To make the Rats and Cats: Cut cookie dough into ¼-inch-thick slices. Make a jagged M–shape cut through the center of each cookie slice as shown in Photo 2, *below middle*. The cookie slice with three points forms the Rat, and the half with two points forms the Cat. Carefully separate the pieces. Place dough on an ungreased baking sheet about 2 inches apart. Bake in a preheated oven for 7 to 9 minutes or until edges are lightly golden. Cool on

wire racks. Decorate as desired, or frost with black-tinted frosting. For the Rat, attach a small piece of string licorice for a tail. Add a candy eye and a slice of a large gumdrop for an ear. Decorate the cat face with small decorative candies.
5. To make the Witches: Cut the cookie dough into ¼-inch-thick slices. Place slices on an ungreased cookie sheet about 2 inches apart. Make a jagged cut through the center of each slice; pull cut pieces apart slightly to form an open mouth as shown in Photo 3, *below right*. Bake in preheated oven for 7 to 9 minutes or until edges are lightly golden. Cool on wire racks. Decorate as desired, or frost with green- or yellow-tinted frosting. Add a candy eye and warts. Shape a witch hat out of rolled large gumdrops and press onto head. Add mouth and hair with edible writing gel. *Makes 30 cookies.*

FRANKENSTEIN'S MONSTER *(shown on page 41)*

Canned vanilla icing
Green food coloring
Graham cracker
Chocolate sprinkles
1   Sathers Cherry Sour Candy
1   small mint patty
1   candy-coated chocolate candy
1   Twizzlers Chocolate Twist candy strip
Black decorating gel
Twizzlers Nibs licorice bits

1. Use green food coloring to tint the icing. Frost the graham cracker with the green icing. Add chocolate sprinkles to the top of the cracker to resemble hair.
2. Use a sharp knife to cut the Cherry Sour Candy in half for the eyes. Place on the cracker as shown. Cut the mint patty in half for eyelids and place each half over the eyes as shown. Use the candy-coated chocolate candy for the nose.
3. Use scissors to cut a 1½-inch piece from the Chocolate Twist candy strip. Cut the strip in half lengthwise and use one piece for the mouth. Press the candy in place.
4. Use the black gel to add eyebrows, pupils, and sutures. Use icing to add licorice bits as neck bolts. *Makes one.*

Skull Head Cake

SKULL HEAD CAKE *(shown on page 40 and above)*
Prep: 1 hour Bake: 25 minutes, 15 minutes for partially filled cake pan
Oven: 350°F

1   2-layer-size package desired flavor cake mix
2   16-ounce cans white frosting
1   tube black decorator frosting*
2   red gum balls
Red chewy fruit-flavored worm-shaped candy

1. Preheat oven to 350°F. Grease and flour two 9-inch round cake pans and one oven-safe 6-inch diameter bowl.
2. Prepare your favorite 2-layer cake mix according to package directions. Pour half of the cake batter into one of the prepared cake pans. Pour 1¼ cups of the batter into the prepared 6-inch bowl. Pour remaining batter into the other 9-inch cake pan. Bake the fuller 9-inch cake pan for 25 to 30 minutes. Bake the bowl for 25 to 30 minutes. Bake the remaining 9-inch cake pan for 15 to 18 minutes. All cakes are done when a toothpick inserted near the center comes out clean. Cool in pans and bowl 10 minutes. Remove cake layers to wire racks and cool completely.
3. Place skull Pattern A, *page 82,* onto the highest 9-inch cake layer. Cut around Pattern A. Place on cake plate. Place skull Pattern B, *page 82,* onto the other 9-inch layer and cut around Pattern B. Spread some of the white frosting onto the cake layer on plate. Place cake layer B and bowl cake appropriately over frosted layer. Hollow out the eyes and nose with a melon baller. Let cake stand for 30 minutes. Combine 1 cup of canned frosting and 3 to 4 teaspoons milk. Frost entire cake and let dry until frosting is set. Frost eyes and nose with black

frosting. Frost cake with remaining white frosting. Attach gum balls into eye sockets with additional black frosting. Pipe teeth and cranium cracks with remaining black frosting. Decorate cake plate and skull with worm candy. *Makes 12 servings.*
*Option: Tint some of the white frosting black using gel or paste food coloring.

HAUNTING HOT CHOCOLATE *(shown on page 42)*
Start to Finish: 15 minutes

1   medium orange
3   cups whole milk
²/₃ cup vanilla-flavored baking pieces or vanilla-flavored candy coating
¹/₈ teaspoon ground nutmeg
1   teaspoon vanilla
Purchased marshmallow ghosts
Whipped cream (optional)
Ground nutmeg (optional)

1. Remove the peel of the orange with a vegetable peeler; set aside.
2. In a medium saucepan, combine ¼ cup of the milk, the vanilla-flavored baking pieces, orange peel, and nutmeg; whisk over low heat until baking pieces are melted. Remove orange peel. Whisk in remaining milk and heat through. Remove from heat. Stir in vanilla.
3. Serve warm in mugs. Add a marshmallow ghost, dollop with whipped cream, and sprinkle with nutmeg if desired. *Makes five 6-ounce servings.*

HOOTIE TWINKIE OWL *(shown on page 37)*

Canned icing (vanilla and chocolate)
2   peppermint LifeSavers candies
2   peach-flavored fruit-circles candies
2   green M&M Minis candies
Sharp knife
2   packages Hostess Twinkies treats
Yellow-and-orange sprinkles mix
4   pieces candy corn
Black licorice twists

1. Referring to the photo on *page 37* and using vanilla icing for "glue," assemble the owl as follows: For the eyes, glue LifeSavers to the fruit circles. Add green M&M Minis for pupils. Use a toothpick to remove any excess icing and to maneuver the pieces. With a sharp knife, cut away one side of each eye; adhere the eyes together along the cut sides.
2. Frost one Twinkie with chocolate icing for the owl tummy and decorate with the sprinkles mix. Cut

one 1×2-inch wing each from two Twinkies, reversing the shapes.

3. Ice the eyes to the head of the body. Add two candy-corn pieces each for the beak and feet. Cut tail feathers and thin eyebrow slivers from black licorice twists; ice in place. Slip the wings next to the body. *Makes one.*

SNAKY SANDWICH *(shown on page 38)*
Prep: 20 minutes   Rise: 1½ hours   Bake: 35 minutes
Cool: 2 hours   Oven: 350°F

1   16-ounce loaf frozen bread dough, thawed
4   ounces sliced mozzarella cheese, diagonally cut in half
4   ounces sliced cheddar cheese, diagonally cut in half
1   3.5-ounce package sliced pepperoni
1   8-ounce can pizza sauce
½   cup red, green, and/or yellow sweet pepper strips
1   strip roasted red sweet pepper
2   pimiento-stuffed olives

1. Place thawed bread dough on a lightly floured surface. Roll into a 22-inch-long rope. Place on a large greased baking sheet forming a snaky S shape. Let rise in a warm place for 1½ to 2 hours or until double in size. Bake in a 350°F oven for 20 minutes or until lightly browned and bread sounds hollow when lightly tapped. Remove from baking sheet to a wire rack. Cool to room temperature.

2. Hollow out the center portion of the loaf about 1 inch deep and 1½ inches wide, leaving about 2 inches on each end of the loaf. Layer cheeses down the center of loaf, pressing cheese slices down into the hollowed portion of the loaf. In a medium bowl, stir together the pepperoni and pizza sauce. Spoon atop the cheese. Top with the strips of sweet pepper. Place on a greased baking sheet and bake in 350°F oven for 15 to 20 minutes or until heated through and cheese is melted.

3. Make a slit in the front of the loaf and insert a roasted red pepper strip for a tongue; insert two pimento-stuffed olives with toothpicks for eyes. *Makes 8 servings.*

CANDY-FILLED WITCHES' HATS
(shown on page 36)
Start to Finish: 45 minutes

Self-sealing plastic bag
1   can chocolate frosting
20   chocolate ice cream cones
Candy corn or assorted small candies
20   2- to 3-inch chocolate cookies
Large green and yellow gumdrops (optional)

1. Fill plastic bag with some chocolate frosting. Seal bag; cut a very small end off one corner of the bag and set aside. For each hat, invert one ice cream cone and fill with about 2 tablespoons candy corn or small candies. Pipe some frosting from bag along bottom edge of cone. Press a cookie against frosting. Carefully invert right side up onto waxed-paper-lined cookie sheet.

2. Decorate outside of cone with small candies, using additional frosting as necessary. Refill frosting bag as needed. If desired, roll out large green and yellow gumdrops on a sugared surface until ⅛ inch thick. Cut into ¼-inch strips. Press green strips around brim of hat and cut smaller pieces from yellow strips to make a buckle; press onto hat. *Makes 20 hats.*

JACK-O'-LANTERN SUGAR COOKIES
(shown on page 39)
Prep: 40 minutes   Bake: 8 minutes/batch
Oven: 350°F

1   18-ounce roll refrigerated sugar cookie
     dough or 24 purchased plain sugar cookies
Orange paste food coloring
1   16-ounce can vanilla frosting
Tubes of colored decorator frosting or gel (red, green, and
     yellow)
Assorted small candies (such as candy corn, candy pumpkins,
     and/or miniature candy-coated milk chocolate pieces)
     and/or licorice

1. If using the refrigerated cookie dough, cut the dough crosswise into ¼-inch slices. Place 1 piece of dough on an ungreased cookie sheet. Reshape the dough into a 2- to 2½-inch circle. Press an indentation into the top of the dough circle to create a pumpkin shape. Repeat with the remaining pieces of dough, spacing the circles about 2 inches apart. Bake in a 350°F oven for 8 to 10 minutes or until edges are lightly browned. Transfer cookies to wire cooking racks. Cool completely.

2. To decorate, add food coloring to purchased vanilla frosting to make orange frosting. Spread frosting on sugar cookies★. Decorate with tube frosting and small candies to make a variety of jack-o'-lantern expressions. Store decorated cookies in an airtight container with waxed paper between layers; serve within 24 hours or freeze up to 3 months. *Makes 24 cookies.*

★ COVER and store any extra frosting in the refrigerator. Let stand at room temperature 30 minutes before using.

Gather the Ghouls

ADAM'S RIBS *(shown on page 75)*
Prep: 25 minutes   Roast: 3 1/2 hours   Broil: 4 minutes
Oven: 275°F

Rub:
1/3   cup dark brown sugar
2   tablespoons ground ginger
1   tablespoon dried thyme, crushed
1   tablespoon garlic salt
1/2   teaspoon ground allspice
1/2   teaspoon cayenne pepper
2   racks pork spareribs (4 1/2 to 5 pounds each)

Glaze:
1 1/2 cups chopped onion
1/2   cup cider vinegar
1/3   cup packed dark brown sugar
Juice and zest of 1 orange
4   cloves garlic, chopped
1   tablespoon ground ginger
2   teaspoons dried thyme, crushed
1/2   teaspoon cayenne pepper
1/8   teaspoon ground allspice

1. In small bowl, stir together all ingredients for dry rub. Divide mixture in half. Pat half onto top side of one rack of ribs; repeat with other half for remaining rack. Preheat broiler. Broil ribs 4 to 5 inches from heat for 2 to 4 minutes per side or until browned. Reduce oven temperature to 275°F. Place ribs on two racks set over two roasting pans. Fill pans halfway with water.

2. Bake, switching pans from top to bottom midway and refilling with water as needed, approximately 3 1/2 hours or until very, very tender.

3. For the Glaze: Combine all ingredients in a medium saucepan. Bring to boiling; reduce heat to low. Simmer for 15 to 20 minutes or until slightly thickened. During the last 20 minutes of roasting time for ribs, brush glaze liberally over ribs.

4. To serve, cut between bones to almost separate. Arrange both racks on a very large cutting board with ribs slightly pulled apart. Place a heart-shaped sweet pepper in between the two racks of ribs, and drive a carving knife through it for dramatic effect and your guests' dining convenience.

5. If you don't have two roasting pans, use the base of your broiler pan. You may need to tuck one end of the ribs under so they'll fit in the pan. *Makes roughly 32 ribs, some quite large, others quite small (6 to 8 servings).*

BLOODY SCARY HARRY *(shown on page 61)*
Start to Finish: 10 minutes

3/4   cup hot-style vegetable juice, chilled
2   tablespoons vodka
2   teaspoons lime juice
Dash celery salt
1/2   cup ice cubes
Ice cubes (optional)
Bottled hot pepper sauce (optional)
Small carrot with top (optional)
Star anise (optional)
Long shreds of beet (optional)

1. In a blender container, combine vegetable juice, vodka, lime juice, and celery salt; add 1/2 cup ice cubes. Cover and blend until smooth. If desired, fill a glass with additional ice cubes. Pour drink into glass. Season to taste with hot pepper sauce if desired.

2. If desired, garnish with a small carrot with green top. For a scary face, press a small piece of star anise into the carrot. For hair, drape long shreds of beet over the carrot top. *Makes 1 drink (about 8 ounces).*

EAT-'EM-UP GHOSTS *(shown on page 65)*
Prep: 35 minutes   Chill: 10 minutes

1   10-ounce bag marshmallows
1/4   cup margarine or butter
6   cups crisp rice cereal
12   ounces vanilla-flavored candy coating
Black licorice candy
Chocolate-flavored sprinkles
Miniature semisweet chocolate pieces

1. In a Dutch oven, combine marshmallows and margarine. Cook and stir over medium-low heat until mixture is melted. Gradually stir in cereal until combined.

2. For each ghost, form 1/2 to 1 cup of the cereal mixture into a ghost shape. Cool thoroughly.

3. In a large saucepan, heat and stir candy coating over medium-low heat until melted. Cool slightly. Dip each ghost into melted candy coating. While coating is still soft, decorate with pieces of licorice, chocolate sprinkles, and/or chocolate pieces to make the eyes, nose, eyebrows, and mouth. Chill for 10 to 15 minutes or until coating is set. *Makes 9 to 12 ghosts.*

BUBBLING BREW (shown on page 62)
Start to Finish: 15 minutes

2 cups water
1 envelope unsweetened lemon-lime-flavored soft drink mix
3/4 cup sugar
Miniature marshmallows
1 1-liter bottle carbonated water, chilled

1. In a medium microwave-safe mixing bowl, heat water for 2 minutes or until hot (140-150°F) but not boiling. Combine soft drink mix and 3/4 cup sugar; stir into hot water. Pour a generous 1/4 cup of the mixture into a tall, narrow glass. Add about 2 tablespoons miniature marshmallows. Stir well. Pour in about 1/2 cup of the carbonated water. *Makes 8 servings.*

CHICKEN LADY FINGERS WITH ROMANIAN ROMESCO DIPPING SAUCE (shown on page 75)
Prep: fingers—15 minutes, sauce—30 minutes

3/4 cup all-purpose flour
1 teaspoon salt
1/2 teaspoon ground black pepper
1 1/2 pounds boneless, skinless chicken breast halves, cut into 1/2-inch by 3-inch strips
1 tablespoon olive oil
1 tablespoon unsalted butter
Smoked Spanish or regular paprika

Romesco Dipping Sauce:
2 large red sweet peppers, halved lengthwise, seeds and membranes removed, and flattened
1 cup day-old crusty bread, cubed
3/4 cup chopped fresh tomato (1 large)
1/3 cup sliced natural almonds, toasted
3 tablespoons sherry vinegar
3 cloves garlic, minced
1/2 teaspoon smoked Spanish or regular paprika
1/2 teaspoon salt
1/4 teaspoon ground black pepper
1/4 cup olive oil

1. Prepare sauce; cover and chill.
2. For the Lady Chicken Fingers: Combine flour, 1 teaspoon salt, and 1/2 teaspoon pepper in a large bowl. Coat chicken strips in flour. Heat 1 tablespoon oil and butter in a large nonstick skillet over high heat. Add chicken strips, one-third at a time, browning well on all sides for 3 to 4 minutes per batch. Dip the end of each chicken strip in ground paprika. Serve with Romesco Dipping Sauce. *Makes 10 servings (about 40 pieces).*
3. For the Romesco Dipping Sauce: Preheat broiler. Place peppers on a broiler pan. Broil peppers 4 to 5 inches from the heat until skins are blacked, turning once.

Remove, stack pieces together, cover with aluminum foil, and let stand 15 minutes. Peel off skins; discard skins. In a blender container, combine peppers, bread, tomato, almonds, vinegar, garlic, paprika, 1/2 teaspoon salt, and 1/4 teaspoon pepper. Cover and blend. Add 1/4 cup olive oil in a steady stream through the top of the blender until mixture is almost smooth. Transfer to a serving bowl or storage container. Cover and chill until serving time. *Makes enough sauce for 10 servings.*

   TIP: You can prepare the sauce ahead of time. Cover and chill up to 3 days.

DEVILS ON HORSEBACK (shown on page 73)
Start to Finish: 1 hour

48 large shrimp (approximately 2 pounds with shells), shelled and deveined
1/4 cup dry white wine
1 teaspoon finely shredded lemon peel
1 to 1 1/2 teaspoons prepared garlic chili sauce
1/2 teaspoon salt
6 strips bacon, quartered (in half lengthwise and then again crosswise), and flattened with the back of a knife to prevent curling
Wooden toothpick

Remoulade:
2/3 cup mayonnaise
2 tablespoons lemon juice
1 tablespoon prepared chili garlic sauce
1 teaspoon salt
2 green onions, finely chopped (both white and green parts)

1. Combine shrimp, wine, lemon peel, 1 to 1 1/2 teaspoons chili garlic sauce, and salt in a non-reactive dish. Marinate for 15 minutes. Remove shrimp and drain on paper towels; discard marinade. Wrap each shrimp in a piece of bacon, securing bacon by skewering shrimp with a wooden toothpick (neck to tail in a half-moon).
2. Preheat broiler. (Position oven rack so the food will be 3 to 4 inches from the heat.) Place shrimp in a single layer on the unheated rack of a broiler pan. Broil, turning twice, until shrimp are opaque and bacon is cooked through and crisp (7 to 9 minutes total).
3. For the Remoulade: Stir together mayonnaise, lemon juice, 1 tablespoon prepared chili garlic sauce, 1 teaspoon salt, and green onions. Cover and chill until serving time.
4. If desired, thread broiled shrimp onto fondue forks or 8- to 10-inch wooden skewers. Serve shrimp with sauce. *Makes 48 shrimp skewers (12 to 16 servings).*

DRACULA'S SODA *(shown on page 63)*
Start to Finish: 5 minutes

2 to 3 scoops vanilla ice cream
Carbonated water, chilled
3 tablespoons fruit punch concentrate, thawed

1. Place ice cream in a tall 10-ounce soda glass. Fill glass with $1/2$ to $3/4$ cup carbonated water. Drizzle thawed fruit punch concentrate over ice cream. Serve immediately. *Makes 1 to 2 servings.*

FROG IN A BLENDER *(shown on page 62)*
Prep: 20 minutes   Chill: 2 hours

2 3-ounce packages lime-flavored gelatin
1 3-ounce package orange-flavored gelatin
1 3-ounce package cherry-flavored gelatin
3 12-ounce cans or bottles lemon-lime carbonated beverage, chilled
1 10-ounce jar red maraschino cherries, drained and stemmed if necessary
Rubber frogs (optional)

1. Prepare each package of gelatin according to package directions, except add only the boiling water called for; stir to dissolve gelatin. Do not add any additional water. Place lime-flavored gelatin in a 4-cup container; transfer orange- and cherry-flavored gelatins to separate 2-cup containers. Cover containers and chill at least 2 hours or until thoroughly set.
2. Cut gelatin into $1/2$-inch cubes. Place about one-third of each flavor of gelatin in a blender container. Add one can or bottle of lemon-lime carbonated beverage. Cover and pulse with 2 or 3 on/off turns or until gelatin has broken up into smaller pieces. Stir in one-third of the cherries. Pour into serving glasses. Repeat with remaining gelatin and carbonated beverage. If desired, garnish with rubber frogs. *Makes 10 to 12 servings.*

GOLDEN BEETLE-JUICE SLUSH *(shown on page 61)*
Prep: 10 minutes   Freeze: 8 hours

1 46-ounce can apricot nectar
1 12-ounce can orange juice concentrate, thawed
2 16-ounce packages unsweetened sliced peaches, thawed
7 12-ounce cans lemon-lime carbonated beverage, chilled

1. In a food processor bowl or blender container, add one third each of the apricot nectar, orange juice concentrate, and peach slices. Cover and blend or process until smooth. Pour into a freezer container. Repeat with the remaining nectar, orange juice, and peaches. Cover and seal mixture. Freeze until firm.
2. Scrape about $1/2$ cup of the mixture into each 10-ounce cup. Add an equal amount of carbonated beverage. Stir to combine. *Makes 20 servings.*

EYES OF NEWT *(shown on page 65)*
Start to Finish: about $1^{1}/2$ hours

1 cup finely crushed, crisp unfrosted sugar cookies
$1/2$ cup toasted hazelnuts or almonds, finely chopped
$1/2$ cup powdered sugar
2 tablespoons light-colored corn syrup
1 tablespoon orange juice
1 tablespoon butter, melted
12 ounces vanilla-flavored candy coating
12 fruit-flavored ring-shaped jelly candies
12 candy-coated fruit-flavored pieces or milk chocolate candy pieces
Red writing gel
Large gumdrops or colorful fruit leather

1. In a medium mixing bowl, combine crushed cookies, nuts, powdered sugar, corn syrup, orange juice, and butter. Stir with a wooden spoon until well mixed.
2. Shape mixture into 2-inch oval shapes, using 1 tablespoon of dough for each. In a small saucepan, melt the candy coating over low heat, stirring until smooth. Remove from heat. Place one oval on the tines of a fork. Holding the fork over the saucepan, spoon melted candy coating over oval until completely covered. Tap bottom of fork on edge of pan to remove excess coating. Use a small metal spatula or table knife to push coated oval onto a sheet of waxed paper. Press a jelly candy in the center of each oval. Affix a candy-coated fruit-flavored piece or milk chocolate candy piece in the center of the jelly candy using a small amount of candy coating. Let stand on waxed paper until coating is set. Decorate with red writing gel, forming eyeballs.
3. Snip large gumdrops into small pieces and press together on a well-sugared surface, 4 at a time. Roll to about $1/8$-inch thickness, combining different colored gumdrops together; sugar generously. Cut into $2^{1}/2$-inch ovals (or cut the fruit leather into $2^{1}/2$-inch ovals). Press two of the ovals around the eyeballs forming eyelids. If not sticky enough, melt additional candy coating and spread on the inside of the eyelids before pressing against the eyeballs. *Makes 12 eyeballs.*

GHOUL-ADE (*shown on page 63*)
Prep: 20 minutes   Freeze: 8 to 24 hours

6   cups unsweetened pineapple juice, chilled
3   cups cold water
1   6-ounce can frozen lemonade concentrate
4   blood orange or orange slices
1   recipe Frozen Hands (see recipe below)

1. For the Punch: Stir together pineapple juice, water, and lemonade concentrate in a punch bowl. Float orange slices and Frozen Hands in punch. *Makes about eight 10-ounce servings.*

2. For Frozen Hands (not shown): Carefully pour cranberry juice cocktail into 2 or 3 clear plastic gloves.★ Fill the gloves so that the fingers can move easily. Tightly seal the gloves with rubber bands. Place on a baking sheet lined with paper towels. Freeze until firm. Use scissors to cut the gloves off the frozen hands. If any fingers break off, just add them to the punch.
★*Note: Be sure to use gloves without powder. Or rinse powdered gloves thoroughly before using.*

HOTTER THAN HADES STEAK AND SALSA BITES (*shown on page 73*)
Prep: steak—25 minutes, salsa—30 minutes
Oven: 350°F

2   cups red and/or yellow grape tomatoes, quartered
1   mango, peeled, pit removed, cut into 1/2-inch pieces
1   avocado, peeled, pit removed, cut into 1/2-inch pieces
6   green onions, white and green parts, chopped (about 1 cup)
1   habanero pepper, seeded and finely chopped
1/2   cup chopped fresh cilantro
2   tablespoons olive oil
Zest and juice from 1 lime
1 1/2 tablespoons whole cumin seeds
1 1/2 tablespoons whole coriander seeds
1   tablespoon packed light brown sugar
1   teaspoon garlic salt
1/2   teaspoon red pepper flakes
1   pound boneless sirloin steak, cut 1 inch thick
1   tablespoon olive oil
Scoop-shaped tortilla chips

1. For the Salsa: Combine tomatoes, mango, avocado, green onions, habanero pepper, fresh cilantro, olive oil, and juice and grated zest of lime in a non-reactive bowl. Let stand 15 minutes at room temperature before serving.

2. For the Steak: Combine cumin and coriander seeds in a small skillet; toast over high heat for 1 to 2 minutes or until fragrant, stirring occasionally. Transfer spices to a spice grinder or mortar (with pestle). Process until finely ground. In a small bowl, combine ground spices, sugar, garlic salt, and red pepper flakes. Rub both sides of steak with oil. Pat half of spice mixture on each side of steak. Preheat broiler. Place steak on the unheated rack of a broiler pan. Broil 4 to 5 inches from the heat for 8 to 9 minutes (for medium-rare doneness), turning once. (For a charcoal grill, grill steak on the rack of an uncovered grill directly over medium coals for 11 to 15 minutes for medium-rare doneness, turning once. For a gas grill, preheat grill. Reduce heat to medium. Place steak on rack over heat and grill as directed above.) Remove meat from broiler or grill. Wrap in foil and let stand 10 minutes. Slice across the grain into very thin slices; cut slices into 2-inch pieces.

3. To serve, place 1 or 2 steak slices in bottom of tortilla chips; top with 1 heaping tablespoon of salsa. *Note: If there are vegetarians at the party, skip the steak and just fill the corn chips with 2 tablespoons of the salsa. Makes 16 servings (4 pieces per serving).*

TIP: Check the ethnic-foods aisle at your local supermarket or the bulk-spice section at a natural foods store for whole cumin and coriander seeds. If you can't find them, substitute 1 tablespoon each ground cumin and coriander in the rub and skip the toasting step.

LAYERED OOZE (*shown on page 63*)
Prep: 15 minutes   Freeze: 4 hours

3   tablespoons frozen grape juice concentrate
1 1/2 cups water
3   tablespoons frozen orange juice concentrate, partially thawed
3   tablespoons frozen limeade concentrate, partially thawed
1   drop green food coloring
2   cups lemon-lime carbonated beverage or carbonated water, chilled

1. In a small bowl, combine grape juice concentrate and 1/2 cup of the water. Pour mixture into a 1 1/2-quart baking dish. Repeat with orange juice concentrate and 1/2 cup water and pour into another 1 1/2-quart baking dish. In a third small mixing bowl, combine limeade concentrate, remaining 1/2 cup water, and 1 drop green food coloring. Pour into a third 1 1/2-quart baking dish. Freeze all dishes for 4 to 24 hours or until firm.

2. Break up ice mixtures slightly with a spoon. Scoop 1/4 of the grape juice mixture into each of four chilled 10-ounce glasses. Scoop 1/4 of the limeade mixture atop grape mixture in each glass. Spoon 1/4 of the orange juice mixture atop limeade mixture in each glass. Gently pour 1/2 cup of the lemon-lime carbonated beverage into each glass. Stir before drinking if desired. *Makes 4 servings.*

UP-FROM-THE-DEPTHS SWAMP PUNCH
(shown on page 60)
Start to Finish: 10 minutes

1   46-ounce can desired berry or apple juice
2   16-ounce packages frozen blueberries
1   12-ounce can frozen grape juice concentrate, thawed
1   2-liter bottle lemon-lime carbonated beverage, chilled
Kumquat Snake (see directions below)

1. In a blender container, add one-third each of the berry juice and blueberries. Cover and blend until nearly smooth. Pour into a chilled large punch bowl. Repeat two more times. Add grape juice concentrate and carbonated beverage. Stir to combine. Skim off excess foam. Add the Kumquat Snake. *Makes 20 servings.*
2. For the Kumquat Snake: Thread a piece of clean dental floss about 24 inches long on a sewing needle. (The sewing needle needs to be longer than the kumquats.) Triple-knot the end of the floss. Thread about 20 kumquats, one at a time, onto the floss. When snake has become about 18 to 20 inches long, rethread the remaining dental floss back through the kumquats as far as possible. Trim off any visible floss. On the first kumquat, press in two whole cloves for the eyes. Use a small sharp knife to make a slit and insert a small piece of maraschino cherry for a tongue.

SHRUNKEN-HEAD MARTINI *(shown on page 61)*
Start to Finish: 10 minutes

Ice cubes
3   ounces vodka
Dash vermouth
Basil leaves
Shrunken-Head Skewer (see directions below)

1. Fill a cocktail shaker with ice; add vodka, vermouth, and two basil leaves. Shake vigorously; strain and pour mixture into a martini glass. Add additional basil leaves. Garnish with a Shrunken-Head Skewer. *Makes 1 serving.*
2. For the Shrunken-Head Skewer: Cook onions in boiling water, covered, for 3 minutes; drain and cool. Remove outer skins from onions. Press whole cloves into onions to form a face. Thread an onion onto a 6-inch skewer with almond-stuffed green olives to form the shrunken head with arms.

TOMBSTONE BROWNIES *(shown on page 64)*

2   15- to 23.5-ounce packages of brownie mix
Aluminum foil
Powdered sugar
Unsweetened cocoa powder
Canned vanilla and chocolate icing
Purple, black, and green food coloring paste
Sealable plastic bags
Oreo cookie crumbs
3   4-inch long wooden skewers
Small sealable container
Shredded coconut

1. Line 8×8×2-inch and 9×13×2-inch pans with foil. Prepare each brownie mix according to package directions and bake one mix in each pan following package directions. Cool in pans. Use edges of foil to lift and transfer brownies to a cutting board. Remove foil. From the 9×13-inch brownie, cut 1¹/2×3-inch rectangles for tombstones. Trim the top corners off of some of the rectangles.
2. Combine powdered sugar and a little cocoa powder and sprinkle mixture over the tombstones. Tint small amounts of vanilla icing with black and purple food coloring paste. Place each tinted icing into a sealable plastic bag. Snip a tiny hole in one corner of each bag and squeeze the icing to decorate the tombstones. Lightly sprinkle tombstones again with the powdered sugar and cocoa mixture.
3. Frost the top and sides of the 8×8-inch brownie with chocolate icing and sprinkle top with cookie crumbs. Insert about half of a 4-inch wooden skewer into the center bottom of each of three brownie tombstones. Position the skewered tombstones on the frosted brownie with the opposite ends of the skewers. (Place the other tombstones on a platter for people to eat right away.)
4. For the grass: Place some green food coloring paste and a few drops of water into a small sealable container; stir to mix. Add coconut, seal the container, and toss the mixture to color the coconut. Sprinkle the green coconut around the base of each tombstone on top of the graveyard brownie. *Makes 24 servings.*

WHITE GHOST *(shown on page 63)*
Start to Finish: 5 minutes

1   6-ounce can unsweetened pineapple juice, chilled
1/4   cup cream of coconut
1   cup lemon-lime carbonated beverage, chilled
1/4   cup half-and-half or milk
1   to 1 1/2 cups crushed ice
Blueberries (optional)

n a blender container, combine pineapple juice,
am of coconut, lemon-lime beverage, half-and-half,
d crushed ice; cover and blend until smooth.
.. Pour into 2 or 3 glasses. If desired, garnish with
blueberries to form a ghostly face through the glass. Serve
immediately. *Makes 2 or 3 servings.*

HERE'S LOOKIN AT YOU *(shown on page 74)*
Start to finish: 1 hour, 15 minutes

½   pound lean ground beef
1   cup fresh bread crumbs
⅓   cup finely chopped onion
1   egg
3   cloves garlic, minced
2   teaspoons Worcestershire sauce
¼   cup onion, finely chopped
3   cloves garlic, minced
¾   teaspoon dried oregano, crushed
½   teaspoon dried basil, crushed
¾   teaspoon salt
½   teaspoon ground black pepper
2   tablespoons olive oil
¼   cup finely chopped onion
3   cloves garlic, minced
¾   teaspoon dried oregano, crushed
½   teaspoon dried basil, crushed
1   28-ounce can crushed tomatoes in puree
4   packages (2.1 oz, 15 pieces) baked mini phyllo shells
2   ounces thinly sliced part-skim mozzarella
30 pitted black olives, halved lengthwise

1. In a medium bowl, mix together ground beef, bread
crumbs, ⅓ cup of the chopped onion, egg, 3 cloves garlic,
Worcestershire sauce, ¾ teaspoon oregano, ½ teaspoon
basil, ¾ teaspoon salt, and pepper. Divide mixture into 60
portions and roll into ball.
2. In a large skillet, heat oil over medium high heat.
Brown the meatballs on all sides, shaking skillet to loosen,
preferably in 2 batches. Remove all meatballs to plate;
reserve. Add remaining ¼ cup onion, 3 cloves garlic, ¾
teaspoon oregano, and ½ teaspoon basil to skillet; cook
and stir for 3 to 4 minutes or until onion is tender. Add
tomatoes and reserved meatballs; bring to a boil. Reduce
heat to low; simmer until the meatballs are cooked
through, 20 to 25 minutes.
3. Preheat oven to 350°F. Place phyllo shells on a baking
sheet. Heat through, 5 to 6 minutes. Place a scant
tablespoon of sauce in each phyllo cup. Top with a
meatball.
4. For eyeball decoration, cut out sixty ¾-inch circles
from sliced mozzarella using aspic or small round cookie
cutter. Place one circle of cheese on each meatball. Cut
out small circles from olive half using a drinking straw.

Place olive circles on top of cheese. Return to oven, 1 to
2 minutes or until cheese just begins to soften. Serve
warm. *Makes 60 eyeballs (30 servings).*

SNAKE EYES *(shown on page 74)*
Start to Finish: 30 minutes

30 large black grapes, dried plum or dried figs, halved either
      vertically or horizontally
1   ounce prosciutto, cut into ½-inch pieces
Freshly ground black pepper
1   8-ounce container mascarpone cheese
1   tablespoon amaretto or almond liqueur
2   teaspoons sugar

1. Trim rounded end of grape so that grape will sit on a
plate without rolling. Using a melon baller or small
spoon, scoop out the insides of the grapes including any
seeds; discard. (If using dried plums or dried figs, simply
cut those in half.) Place one piece of prosciutto inside
each piece of fruit. Sprinkle with black pepper. In small
bowl, stir together mascarpone, amaretto, and sugar.
2. Place cheese mixture in a pastry bag fitted with a
small round tip. (Or transfer mixture to a heavy-duty
plastic food storage bag; snip off one corner). Pipe filling
into fruit halves, mounding into semi-circle. Decorate
with various trimmings of grapes for pupils or sliced
almonds. Chill until served. *Makes 60 eyes (30 servings).*

RED EYE SPECIALS *(shown on page 74)*
Start to Finish: 30 minutes

30 small plum tomatoes (about 2 inches long)
⅔   cup purchased pesto
2   containers (6 oz. each) bocconcini (mini fresh mozzarella balls)
About 30 pitted black olives
2   green onions

1. Cut tomatoes in half crosswise. Trim off the end of
each half so that tomato cup will set upright. Scoop out
insides of tomato with small spoon and/or melon baller.
Spoon ½ teaspoon pesto into each tomato cup. Drain
bocconcini and cut each piece in half.
2. Use end of drinking straw to scoop out a little dent in
center of the rounded side of each bocconcini. Use same
straw to cut out "pupils" from olive halves. Place half a
bocconcini in each tomato cup. Place olive inside the hole
for pupil.
3. For eyelashes, using scissors, cut the green top of
the green onion into ¼-inch pieces. Snip the onion ring
so that you have a narrow strip. Use scissors to make multiple
cuts almost to edge of strip. Tuck eyelashes into gap between
cheese and tomato with toothpick. *Makes 60 eyes (30 servings).*

Better Homes and Gardens®
Creative Collection®

Editorial Director
Gayle Goodson Butler

Editor in Chief Deborah Gore Ohrn

Executive Editor Karman Wittry Hotchkiss

Managing Editor Kathleen Armentrout

Contributing Editorial Manager Heidi Palkovic

Contributing Design Director Tracy DeVenney

Copy Chief Mary Heaton
Contributing Copy Editor Dave Kirchner
Proofreader Joleen Ross
Administrative Assistant Lori Eggers

Publishing Group President
Jack Griffin

Chairman and CEO William T. Kerr
President and COO Stephen M. Lacy

In Memoriam
E. T. Meredith III (1933–2003)

Contributors

Designers
Glenda Aldrich: pages 11 (right), 12 (bottom),
   and 19.
Laura Collins: pages 40 and 41.
Lori Hellander: page 25.
Ann Holtz: pages 38 (top), 68, 69, and 70.
Tami Leonard: page 64.
Diana McMillen: pages 7 (top), 9, 15 (right),
   and 29.
Matthew Mead: front cover, pages 6, 13, 16, 17, 22,
   23, 24, 31, 32, 66, 67, 71, and back cover (left and
   middle right).
Vicki Nail: pages 44, 45, 47, and 52.
Carol Schalla: pages 7 (top), 9, 15 (right), and 29.
Kenneth Seiling: page 28.

Food Stylist
Diana Nolin: pages 38 (bottom), 60, 61 (left), 62, 63, 64,
   65 (top), 72, 73, 74, and 75.

Recipe Development
Lisa Bell: pages 72, 73, 74, and 75.

Photographers
King Au: pages 49, 50, and 51.
Marty Baldwin: page 7 (bottom), 25, 27, 61 (left), 63, and 64.
Monica Buck: page 16.
Bob Coyle: page 12.
Reed Davis: pages 6, 22, 23, 24, 31, 32, 66, 67, and 71.
M. Lorin Gross: pages 13 and 17.
Hopkins Associates: pages 18 and 20.
Pete Krumhardt: pages 7 (top), 9, 15 (right), 29, 39, 40, and 41.
Scott Little: pages 8, 37 (right), 42 (top), 42 (bottom), 43, 54 (top),
   61 (right), 65 (bottom), 72, 73, 74, and 75.
Andy Lyons: pages 10, 21, 36–37, 38 (bottom), 48, 54 (bottom 3),
   55, 57, 60, 62, and 65 (top).
Blaine Moats: pages 11 (right) and 12 (bottom).
Greg Scheidemann: pages 38 (top), 44, 45, 47, 52, 68, 69, and 70.
Perry Struse: pages 28 and 56.
Jason Wilde: pages 26, 30, and 33.